THE
HORSE
IN MYTH AND LEGEND

THE

HORSE

IN MYTH AND LEGEND

SOPHIE JACKSON

To my nannies: Olive, Lily and Pauline,
because I remember.

First published 2006

Tempus Publishing Limited
The Mill, Brimscombe Port,
Stroud, Gloucestershire, GL5 2QG
www.tempus-publishing.com

British Library Cataloguing in Publication Data.
A catalogue record for this book is available from the British Library.

ISBN 0 7524 3830 1

Typesetting and origination by Tempus Publishing Limited
Printed in Great Britain

CONTENTS

INTRODUCTION

The horse is an animal of power and speed, grace and elegance; it has been the subject of poetry, art and literature; for the Celts, Vikings and Saxons it was associated with magic and the gods; for later generations it was a symbol of power, a status symbol. Further on, it was the farmer's friend, and an integral part of the blacksmith's trade.

For the horse is one of the earliest domesticated animals along with the dog, and like the dog it is loyal, obedient and trusting. Strong bonds can grow between a rider and their horse, particularly as the horse can live for many years. For others the horse was a practical animal, it drew carts and ploughs, it provided transport and for the less law-abiding, a speedy getaway when it was necessary.

Today we usually only see working horses at public demonstrations, it is a rare sight indeed to pass a field and see a horse pulling a plough, otherwise our only glimpse of a horse is as our cars carefully pass

Along with the dog, the horse is one of the oldest domesticated animals and up until relatively recently it was an essential animal for transport and farming. The horse's intelligence, loyalty and gentle nature have rightfully earned it a place alongside the dog as man's most trusted companion. (Early twentieth-century postcard 'It's nearly Dinnertime')

a rider on a country lane. Much of what the horse meant to our ancestors has been forgotten, we worship the engine rather than the equine. Centuries ago, so much magic and mystery surrounded the horse, so much marvel and majesty; there were superstitions, traditions, rituals and legends. To truly understand what the horse meant to our ancestors we must understand the mythology behind the animal.

We may no longer need the horse to pull a coach or to prepare a field for planting, but there is so much more to the animal than just this practical aspect. From deities and legends to sacrifices and ghosts, the horse has not only fed the human imagination but been an intrinsic part of early religions. We may not still believe that horsehairs can turn into eels, but many people would swear that a horseshoe is extremely lucky. There is far more to the mystery of the horse than a glimpse out of a car window or a glance into a field can tell us; behind these gentle animals there is a history of bloodshed, black arts and demons. There is much more to the horse than meets the eye.

ONE

PRIMITIVE CHALK HORSES

THE UFFINGTON HORSE

Perched on the side of a scarp on the Berkshire Downs, the Uffington White Horse is distinctive in its strangely exaggerated and stylised form. Its strange beak-like mouth and deeply incised ears that almost sever the head from the neck remind us of a remote and ancient time. The elongated horse gallops across the grass, its antiquity not in doubt, though over the course of many centuries its exact appearance has altered and changed. Drawings made during the nineteenth century show a slightly different horse, the head is solid without an eye and the back has two strange indentions, which some suggest the horse once carried a rider. That the horse has changed over the long course of its lifetime is only to be expected; it is carved into an organic material, grass and soil, which over time will naturally cover the brilliant white chalk that has been exposed to form the

The Uffington horse in Wiltshire is perhaps the oldest chalk hill figure dating to the late Bronze Age, its strange stylised appearance and 'beak' make it stand out on the rolling green hillsides. But it remains uncertain why it was cut and who originally designed and carved the majestic horse. (Photograph taken by Paul Newman and used with his kind permission)

body, thus the horse is regularly 'scoured', that is re-cut, which also results in slight changes to shape and form, particularly if the horse has been neglected for some time.

But who originally cut the horse and for what reason? The first question is the simpler to answer; analysis of silts taken from within the cutting gives a date of close to 3,000 years ago, placing the horse in the late Bronze Age or early Iron Age. Other evidence helps to confirm the date, from ancient coins and other archaeology finds that show similar, though not identical horses. Bearing in mind that the Uffington horse has clearly changed over many centuries of cutting and scouring these coins and other decorated objects still show a striking likeness in their artistic style and concept. Looking at an Iron Age coin impressed with a trotting horse it is easy to imagine that this was how the White Horse's creators envisaged him. The horses on these coins are disjointed, their bodies and limbs separated, their noses beak-like, their tails a single thin line and they all face right. With all this evidence there seems no doubt that the Uffington horse is the oldest chalk horse still in existence.

Yet, still we wonder, why does it exist? There have been many theories; unfortunately several of these rely on the horse being younger than we now know it to be. The horse is variously attributed to Hengist (reputed to be one of the first Saxon chieftains), King Alfred the Great and later it was considered to be a representation of St George's horse. Hengist was said to have cut it because he had a white horse on his standard, King Alfred was said to have ordered the horse to be created to honour his victory over the Danes at Ashdown in AD 871. Of course with the new dates none of these theories can possibly explain the horse's original cutting and yet the debate of why the Uffington horse was cut has come up with no solid answers. It is suggested that the horse is a landmark, designed to show travellers which route to take, but this is considered an unlikely candidate. More dramatically it is claimed the horse was carved to commemorate a great victory in battle, now forgotten; if this is true perhaps it later became confused with the victories of Hengist or Alfred? Lastly and perhaps most convincingly it is argued that the horse is a totem, cut into the radiant white chalk to indicate to all around that this was home to a certain tribe. The White Horse is close to Uffington Castle, an early Iron Age camp, it seems very likely that the inhabitants of this enclosure created the horse to mark their land particularly as festivities associated with the scouring of the horse took place within its ramparts. But however much we speculate, for the time being we simply do not have the evidence to conclusively prove any of these theories. The White Horse remains an enigma that still fascinates those who visit it today as once it must have impressed and amazed our ancestors who saw this mighty beast striding across the hills. Whether totem or victory tribute no wonder this part of Berkshire has become know as the Vale of the White Horse.

THE WESTBURY HORSE

Unlike its distant neighbour of Uffington there is no conclusive proof that the Westbury horse is of ancient standing, but debate still rages about its true origins, made especially harder since the horse has been dramatically re-sculpted. This occurred in 1778 when Mr Gee, a steward for Lord Abingdon, took it upon himself to radically redraw the horse, creating the creature that is seen today. The modern horse is a stoic creature standing calmly on the pitched slope of Bratton Down, Wiltshire, staring across the landscape with one large triangular eye, a perfect representation of a horse unlike the impressionistic Uffington steed. But Mr Gee's artistic work has been soundly criticized for destroying the older beast that once graced the hill.

A picture of the older horse as surveyed by the eighteenth-century topographer Gough, appeared in his edition of Camden's *Britannia*.

The Westbury White Horse stands prominently on a hill in Wiltshire. Some debate remains as to whether the current horse, constructed in 1778, was carved on top of a much older hill figure. If there was once an older horse it has since been eradicated by the present occupant of the hillside. (Early twentieth-century postcard 'The White Horse, Westbury')

His study was done in 1772 and shows a bizarre creature, clumsily executed, more of a worn-out nag than the elegant steed that has taken his place. The horse is strangely elongated with spindly legs. He has two ears (unlike his successor's singular ear) and one bulbous eye that stands slightly proud of the head and gives him a comical, dazed look. Beneath him there is a line to suggest male genitals, but the most remarkable feature of this horse is his tail, which sweeps down and then up and ends in a crescent shape.

Much importance is placed on this tail and many point to it as proof of the horse's antiquity. Revd W.C. Plenderleath, who wrote about the Wiltshire horses in the nineteenth century, was convinced that the crescent represented the moon, which often featured above horses on Iron Age coins and that inexpert scourers had mistakenly assumed it to be part of the tail and so had linked the two together. He went on to associate the horse with the Welsh fertility goddess Ceridwen, a considerable leap considering the lack of evidence.

Further argument for an Iron Age date for the horse comes from its position near the Iron Age encampment of Bratton Castle. This has also led to another King Alfred legend. Alfred seems to have been preoccupied with building white horses if the numerous stories connecting him with their creation are to be believed. As in the case of the Uffington horse, Alfred was said to have commissioned the Westbury White Horse after another victory over the Danes in AD 878. At this time Alfred's biographer records that the Danes were terrorising Somerset, Hampshire and Wiltshire and Bratton Castle is thought of as their stronghold, which Alfred lay siege to and eventually captured. He then ordered the white horse to be created on the slope below. A tidy story but with no real supportive evidence.

Though the old arguments will probably never be laid to rest it seems evermore likely that the Westbury horse is not in fact ancient. At the earliest it probably dates to the beginning of the eighteenth century and was first recorded by Revd F. Wise in 1742. It is probably a wealthy landowner's folly, built in a deliberately archaic and clumsy style to convince people that it was ancient.

But the argument will not rest. T.C. Lethbridge claimed he could see another ancient horse in the grass behind the current equine. He drew a picture of this 'lost' horse and created a beast far more fantastical than the original Westbury horse. This steed appears to have two long tusks, armour on its back and a saddle blanket. He reproduced a drawing of this forgotten horse in his book *Gogmagog*. Few people consider this a real find, rather that it is one man trying to piece together a horse from the natural lines and contours of the hill.

There seems no reason to assume there was ever an Iron Age horse on the hillside, only the wild imaginings of people who so badly desired another primitive horse roaming their countryside.

THE RED HORSE OF TYSOE

There have been numerous horses carved onto a hillside overlooking the village of Tysoe and all are now lost irretrievably as the area has been ploughed, overgrown and now replanted with trees. But there is evidence that this hillside visible from the battlefield of Edgehill once carried horses as grand as the Uffington stallion, leading to the land being known as the Vale of the Red Horse.

Until the 1960s the earliest horse carvings were either unknown or considered just another local story as there seemed to be no evidence in the land to suggest the presence of the figures. Two men, G. Miller and K.A. Carrdus, decided to try and find this lost horse. Beginning by photographing the location they thought the horse occupied at different times of the year and with filters on the camera

This photograph from the 1960s is one of the original groundwork pictures taken by Graham Miller whilst he was searching for the Red Horse of Tysoe. The photograph was accidentally enlarged when it was developed, which enabled Miller to see the faint outline of the horse just visible in the grass on the top of the hill, where hedges ran along. Without this picture it is unlikely the Tysoe horses would ever have been found. (Photograph taken by Graham Miller and used with his kind permission)

they could clearly make out changes in the colour of the grass, which indicated the presence of something beneath. The patterns seemed to form a large horse, galloping across the hill, with a smaller companion running ahead. This smaller horse was considered the first's foal, and the area containing the 'mare and colt' now had a soil resistivity survey conducted across it. The results corresponded with the photographic evidence and it seemed that Miller and Carrdus had found their horse.

Trenches were dug across the ear and neck of the horse and the clay within was found to be compacted, also red iron oxide silt was found that contrasted sharply with the yellow clay of the soil. This bright red material, used to infill the trenches, would have given the horse its rich colouring which made it so unusual.

It is thought the horse was built by the Angles who, around AD 600, had settled in the Stour Valley. Though, once again, Hengist appears as the possible perpetrator there is no more evidence linking him to this horse than any other. The horse is said to represent fecundity, the foal gambolling before it emphasizing its fertility and links with the god Tiw. The name Tysoe means 'spur of land dedicated to Tiw' and, as the god of both war and agriculture, the horse was sacred to him. Horses were sacrificed to Tiw during spring rituals, which also involved horse-racing and the devouring of horse flesh. This perhaps explains the names of two hills lying north of Tysoe, Spring and Sunrising, and confirms that the hills were used as part of festivities to celebrate the first equinox of the year. Later these pagan rituals became muddled with Christianity and, though it is unclear why, Tiw's celebrations became the Palm Sunday festivities, when the scouring of the horse continued on, though no longer with the same significance.

Around the same time as the first investigations of the mare and foal, A.G. Wildman, claimed he had not only found another horse on the hillside, but an actual representation of Tiw bearing a whip, which he supposed showed his superiority over the horse. Tiw was accompanied by a bird-like creature and standing above an indistinct mass that Wildman later considered was a slaughtered animal. There is little supportive evidence for this claim, though the figure may be composed from the overgrown outlines of later horses.

Despite the horse and foal's earlier cultural significance, or maybe because of it, the animals became neglected and vanished. A third horse was cut to replace them but lacked the elegance and size of the originals. It was lumbering and rather clumsy, though interestingly is said to have had a tail like a lion's and certain drawings show a tail very reminiscent of that belonging to the Westbury horse. It seems this was the horse mentioned in Camden's *Britannia* of 1607 and also by Sir William Dugdale, an English antiquarian, in 1657. It was this same horse that aroused Revd F. Wise's contempt in 1742 when he called it, 'vastly inferior to the Uffington Horse'.

Its 'inferiority' did not prevent this later horse from attaining an origin legend as fantastical as those attributed to other hill figures. The story goes that during the War of the Roses Richard, Earl of Warwick, was fighting at Towton, Yorkshire on Palm Sunday, 1641. He was heavily outnumbered and defeat looked to be soon at hand, when Richard, in a moment of rash cruelty, vaulted from his horse and proceeded to drive his sword through his poor steed. He declared as the poor creature died that he would fight shoulder-to-shoulder alongside his men. This reckless act seems to have boosted morale, Richard's men rallied and won the battle. To honour the victory a horse was cut on a hill at Tysoe, or so the legend goes, unfortunately there is no reason to connect Richard with the Vale of the Red Horse and certainly no reason to conclude that the horse was built to commemorate his victory at Towton. More likely the horse was built as a reminder of the previous hill horses which had fallen into neglect.

But this horse too was not to last. It was ploughed over in 1800 when the owner of Sunrising Inn acquired Sunrising Farm. He later noticed a drop in his takings as he no longer had the financial boost of thirsty workers buying drinks from him during the Palm Sunday scouring festivities. To advertise his establishment and also to encourage back the drinkers he cut another horse, but this too has subsequently been grassed over and nothing remains of the grand herd that once chased down the hillside, a celebration of ancient rites and rituals that once gave this beautiful place the title of Vale of the Red Horse.

THE WANDLEBURY HORSE

The Wandlebury Horse, or rather collection of hill figures, as the horse only forms part of a mural, is a controversial matter. The evidence for the large scene of Celtic gods is provided by an unorthodox archaeologist, T.C. Lethbridge, whose findings have not been confirmed by modern methods such as resistivity meters and magnometers. In his book *Gogmagog* he provides an interesting argument for the existence of the hill figures, but even the official Wandlebury websites and tourist pamphlets refrain from agreeing with the findings, preferring to leave the subject open to debate.

The site for this strange story is the Gog Magog Hill in Wandlebury, Cambridge. The name alone has been cause for heated discussions; those who follow T.C. Lethbridge's view consider the hills to be named after gods, Gog male, Magog female. But the names have a far more complicated history than this. The original Gog was in the bible, the chief prince of Meshech and Tubal who came from the land of Magog and it was prophesied that he would attack Israel. By the medieval period the writer Geoffrey of Monmouth (d. 1154) was

One of the most controversial hill figures was excavated by T.C. Lethbridge in Cambridge, Suffolk. His techniques were unorthodox and his findings greatly criticised. He claimed the goddess Epona riding a horse was carved on the hillside and later unearthed other supposed gods. His figures were eventually covered up after much debate and later archaeological investigations have been unable to discover evidence of the hill figures. (Author's own drawing)

using the names of prince and land as one. Gogmagog (Goemagot) had become a giant terrorising parts of England. Somehow, using a complicated system of imaginative leaps and suppositions, Lethbridge takes these two figures and comes up with a Celtic god and goddess, though only after he has unearthed 'figures' on the hillside which he needs to name. The truth is no one is entirely certain why the hill is named Gog Magog. Richard Coates even suggested in a paper on the linguistics of the Wandlebury giants that the name is actually very similar to hodmedod or hodmandod, a colloquial term for snails. It is interesting to note that in some early references to the hill it is called Hogmagog, and that the concentric rings of the Iron Age fort that once stood on the hill resemble the way a snail shell twists.

Despite all these dead ends and inconclusive suppositions there is some evidence that a hill figure once graced the hillside, though unfortunately it appears to have been a giant and not a horse. The earliest specific mention of the Wandlebury giant comes from Bishop Joseph Hall in 1605, when he compares another giant, 'All Paunch, who was of incredible Height of body,' to the Cambridge figure, saying All Paunch was, 'not like him whose Picture the Schollers of Cambridge got to see at Hogmagog Hills...' So at this time a figure existed on the hillside but was considered small, at least by Bishop Hall. Another mention comes thirty-five years later from John Layer, an historian of Cambridge whose view was 'I could never learn how these hills came to be called Gogmagog Hills, unless it were from a high and mighty portraiture of a giant wch the Schollers of Cambridge cut upon the turf or superficies of the earth within the said trench...but it is now of late discontinued.' Yet another Cambridge antiquary recalled seeing the giant as a boy in 1724, 'I went with one of them [his parents] to Cambridge, the road from Baberham lying through the camp, [they] always used to stop and show me and my Brother and Sisters the figure of the giant carved on the turf.' These accounts all indicate that once a giant was carved on the hillside within the trenches of the long disappeared hill fort. There were also legends of two gods being buried in a chalk pit and a golden chariot lying hidden somewhere near Wandlebury.

With all this in mind Lethbridge decided to try and find the lost giant, though he did not examine the hill fort where the giant had been reported, but picked a spot overlooked by Sawston. He used a very unusual technique to make his discovery whereby he drove an iron bar into the ground and where it hit soft soil he considered this to indicate a trench, possibly originally part of a chalk figure. In each hole he made that hit such a soft patch he placed a stick which would eventually form the outline. He quickly began to make discoveries, the first being a very peculiarly shaped pattern with a rounded top that Lethbridge compared to a bowler hat. He sent a sketch to Sir Thomas Kendrick at the British Museum and the reply was astonishing; Kendrick said the pattern was the rear quarter of a walking animal and even suggested it could be a white horse. Anyone looking at these strange lines reproduced in Lethbridge's book may find it difficult to come to a similar conclusion, but Lethbridge was convinced and spurred on to find more.

As his 'soundings' continued with the bar, more of the horse emerged, as did a figure riding the weirdly contorted beast. Another sketch was drawn and this time sent to Sir Cyril Fox, author of *Archaeology of the Cambridge Region*. The reply that came back was even more stunning, 'Female with two horses, probably Epona. Congratulations.' Epona was a Celtic horse deity who was adopted by the Roman Cavalry when they invaded Britain (see Chapter Two). She is sometimes represented as a horse but more commonly riding one. Now here on Gog Magog hill was this goddess along with her horses; Lethbridge could hardly believe what he was uncovering and began imagining all sorts of elaborate reasons for her presence. Looking at the drawings however it can be difficult to make out the horses, though the figure above them has a face which instantly turns it into a person. This person was initially considered male but when a nipple was uncovered the figure suddenly became female; as for her steeds they are strangely elongated, beak-headed monsters with none of the grace nor simplicity of lines which the Uffington horse possesses. The equines are in fact such a jumble of lines that is hard to imagine how anyone ever drew them like that in the first place.

Lethbridge continued on with increased enthusiasm. Soon two more figures were added to the group: a sun god standing in front of the horse and figure and a warrior with raised sword chasing behind. These figures appeared of later construction than the goddess and horse. Epona had now become Magog in Lethbridge's mind, she symbolised the moon chasing on the tail of the sun. He excavated the goddess and for a time she stood boldly on the hill with her horses. But doubts were beginning to be voiced. Could Lethbridge's techniques be trusted? Was he actually finding hill figures and why were they in a different place to those mentioned in earlier texts? Experts derided the findings; even an eminent archaeologist and friend of Lethbridge's considered the finds false. It was decided amongst archaeologists that Lethbridge had been fooled by geological features caused during the Ice Age, along with plough marks, water gullies and pits caused by trees falling. Looking at the convoluted system of lines that make up these 'figures' this could well be the case, many naturally occurring contours and markings in the landscape can look like an animal or person, it only takes a little bit of imagination. Perhaps most damning is that later surveys of the hill with various pieces of equipment could find no evidence of hill figures. However, there may once have been a giant on the hill but cut within the old fort ditches; if this is the case then it would not have been of great antiquity as carving a figure within a working fort is not practical nor would it have been very visible. Perhaps a giant was carved when the hill fort only existed as rings in the grass, but sadly it seems unlikely that there was ever a chalk horse striding across Wandlebury.

OTHER CHALK HORSES

This chapter has been mainly concerned with horses that have or may have had origins going back many centuries, but to conclude without at least mentioning the wealth of other white horses that have at one time raced across the countryside would be neglectful. They may be more recent in date, little more than two centuries old or even younger, and they were not built for the same reasons as their predecessors, but they still have a place in our cultural heritage.

Wiltshire seems to have more than its fair share of horses, eight are mentioned in the tourist guides and there was once a ninth. The Cherhill Horse is second oldest (Westbury being the first) being created in 1780 under the direction of Dr Christopher Alsop who shouted directions through a megaphone to workmen who positioned flags in the turf until they formed a reasonable impression of a horse. It was then cut out and the eye embedded with glass bottles to sparkle in the sunlight, unfortunately none remain. Though the horse lies near an ancient earthwork it is not thought that there was ever an earlier horse on the site.

In 1804 the Marlborough horse was created by the boys of the local school, run by a Mr Greaseley. The rather naïve creature was designed by William Canning of the Manor House; after he had pegged out the horse the boys removed the turf and filled the figure in with lumps of chalk. The horse was regularly scoured until Mr Greasely died in 1830, the tradition was only renewed in 1873 when Captain Reed of Marlborough, an ex-pupil of Greaseley's school, took up the task.

The Alton Barnes Horse was paid for by Mr Robert Pile of Manor Farm. He gave twenty pounds to journeyman John Thorne to peg out and cut the horse, but after only quickly sketching the design on the turf, John Thorne employed a second man, John Harvey, to do the digging and then absconded with the money. Mr Pile had to finish the horse himself. John Thorne was eventually caught and hanged for other crimes.

Broad Town Horse and Hackpen Horse lie relatively close to each other. The first was probably cut around 1864 by William Simmonds, a local farmer. He intended to keep enlarging the horse at each scouring but he did not stay at the farm long enough to do this. The Hackpen Horse is said to have been cut by the parish clerk of Broad Hinton in 1838 to commemorate the Coronation of Queen Victoria in 1837.

There have been two Pewsey White Horses, the original was created in 1785 by Mr Robert Pile of Alton Barnes fame, but has long since vanished. The current horse was designed by Mr George Marples to celebrate the Coronation of King George VI in 1937. Another horse that vanished and was then replaced is the Devizes Horse, originally begun in 1845 by apprentice shoemakers it was never finished and was eventually grassed over. The current horse lies a mile from the first and was cut for the millennium.

(1738) THE WHITE HORSE OF KILBURN.—This figure was formed in November, 1857, by Mr. Thomas Taylor, a native of the village of Kilburn, in the valley below. The land on which the horse stands is (or was) the property of Mr. Dresser, of Kilburn Hall. Length, 180 feet; height, 80 feet; quantity of land covered, 3 roods; and to make a fence round would enclose two acres. Six tons of lime were used to give his skin the requisite whiteness, and 33 men were at work upon him on the 4th of November, the day on which he was completed. This figure was merely cut out to gratify the whim of the projector, not to commemorate any remarkable event. The following references appeared in a contemporary :—The White Horse of Kilburn, near Thirsk, was formed to commemorate a legend of a horse trainer, who was said to have been borne down a precipice, along with his steed and killed.

During the eighteenth and nineteenth centuries there was a revival in chalk figures and many were carved, some to commemorate important events, others just for pure pleasure. The Kilburn Horse created by Thomas Taylor in 1857 is a typical example of the many horses that were being created during that century. (1904 postcard)

The final horse of Wiltshire is now lost. It lay north-west of Marlborough on the Rockley Down and had been hidden for years until the field was ploughed and the horse revealed in the furrows. There is no record of its cutting but it seems unlikely that it is older than the early nineteenth century, though a theory that it was carved to mark the Battle of Barbury, (AD 556) has been put forward. More probably it was carved at the instruction of the owners of Rockley Manor.

Outside of Wiltshire other white horses of Britain are as follows: The Mormond White Horse in Aberdeenshire appears to be the only horse hill figure in Scotland. Legend has it that it was carved by one of the Fraser family, lairds of nearby Strichen, to honour a favourite horse around 1775. The name of this laird is not known but legend has it that he was so eccentric that he died of exasperation when he could not get the horse's legs to look accurate from every angle. Unusually the horse is made of white quartz native to the region and is easier to maintain than the chalk horses.

The Osmington Horse in Dorset was carved in 1815 and represents George III riding a horse. It is said to have been carved to celebrate the king's patronage of Weymouth as the horse looks out over Weymouth Bay and is clearly intended to be seen from the sea. It is variously said that a single soldier or group of soldiers or even engineers created the horse, but it seems no one knows the true identity of this mighty beast's designer.

There have been two Littlington Horses. The older horse was cut in 1838, possibly to commemorate the Queen's Coronation like the Hackpen horse, but later fell into disrepair and vanished. The current horse was built around 1924, by whom no one seems to remember. It is said to act as a memorial to a girl who died when her horse threw her.

In Yorkshire grazes the Kilburn Horse, built in 1857 by Thomas Taylor a successful grocer who is said to have visited the Uffington horse when it was being scoured and was inspired to give his native county its own monument. Thirty-three men are said to have worked on the horse and six tons of lime were needed to initially whiten it.

The Woolbury Horse in Hampshire, built 1859, is said to be in remembrance of a traveller and his horse who were set upon by robbers at that location. The traveller was killed, his horse galloped to Woolbury where it died from its injuries. The horse is picked out in flints, which makes its shape rather vague, it is the smallest hill horse in the country.

Finally there must be a mention for the Black Horse of Bush Howe. This strange apparition is said to appear on the hills in the Pennines north of Sedbergh when the clouds lift. It is said to look like a stallion marked out in black shale and some suggest it represents a dobbie, a river entity that could change shape; others think the horse is a marker used by smugglers entering Morecombe Bay. It is really not clear what this horse is; perhaps it is simply an effect of the light? Some refuse to acknowledge its existence and it remains unmarked on maps and overlooked in local publications.

TWO

HORSE DEITIES

THE HORSE CULT

The horse was an integral part of the early religions of Britain; Epona and Rhiannon were horse deities, Arawn the god of the underworld rode a pale horse whilst his Irish female counterpart, Clíodna, presided over horse racing, and it was believed that the dead rode to the afterlife on horses (in Norse mythology it was also believed that warriors killed in battle were taken to Valhalla by the horse riding Valkyries). When the Irish voyager Maeldun sailed the oceans, amongst the many wondrous and yet deadly things he found was an island where a demonic horse race was being carried out and an island of fierce, giant blacksmiths. The supernatural Etain Macha, the daughter of an Ulster prince, was forced to take part in a race by an Irish king because her husband had boasted she could outrun his finest horses. She was heavily pregnant and died on the finish line giving birth to twins after winning the race. She was probably a horse deity. Twins and horses had a divine link; the hero Cuchulain was born at the same time as twin foals who became his two fine war horses, the Black of Saingliu and the Grey of Macha. The Grey had clairvoyant powers and wept bloody tears foretelling her master's demise. The similar names of the horse and Etain Macha show that Cuchulain is linked with horse deities.

Such a plethora of gods and goddesses, divine heroes and mystical steeds, reveals how sacred an animal the horse was to our ancestors. It was a beast of burden, it provided transport and it was a creature possessed of healing powers and the ability to predict the future. In times of desperation it could be a source of food. But most importantly it was an earthly link between the Celts and their gods. It was never more important than during the coronation rituals of the Irish kings. A white mare would be brought amongst those gathered for the ritual, she represented a goddess of the land and fertility and the king had to be bonded with her so that he too might be linked with the land and serve his tribe well. Once the mare had been brought forward so the king must enter, he came in on all fours declaring himself nothing better than a beast and then proceeded to act like a stallion and mate with the mare, thus 'marrying' king, deity and land together. It was also an act designed to demonstrate the king's virility, an important issue to the tribe as the king's health and sexual potency would be reflected on the tribe's well-being.

The white mare had now served her role and she was slaughtered and her flesh prepared in a broth bath that the king sat in and lapped up. Not only had he mated with the goddess but now he devoured her flesh, becoming her, and his royal ascension was now ratified

This demonic horse head with jagged teeth and bridle glares down from an arched door in Wissett Church, Suffolk. Such carvings remain in many churches and houses demonstrating that pagan influence lingered in Britain even after Christianity's arrival. Perhaps this horse represents Puca, an old god who would change into a horse to cause mischief, or perhaps a Saxon demon that had become incorporated into the new religion.

and final. This strange practice, which goes against many other old superstitions and religious doctrines against eating horse flesh, was being performed until the twelfth century, much to the disgust of those who reported it and to the Christians in Ireland who were trying to rout out such purely pagan practices. Today we consider such a ritual bizarre and brutal, but to ancient cultures it made sense; what better way for a king to bond with his goddess than to mate with her effigy?

ANCIENT EPONA

Epona was a horse goddess, an earth mother, a symbol of fertility and of the Roman cavalry. Epona is a Celtic deity, and it is possible that originally she was simply seen as a mare, a symbol of fecundity. Perhaps some of the ancient horse carvings of Britain represent Epona in her equine form, as may Celtic coins. Her original image as a horse gradually changed and soon Epona was a woman riding a horse, perhaps showing a change in early religion, from the people perceiving themselves as one with animals, or at least interlinked with them, to becoming masters of the natural world and able to tame the wild. She was still linked with fertility, and sometimes a foal was depicted running beside her to accentuate this feature of her persona, but she was also a figure of nature, she had birds that flew around her and this links her to a role as an 'earth mother', or nature goddess.

As time moved on Epona became a more general horse deity particularly once she became adopted and worshipped in Rome. Her

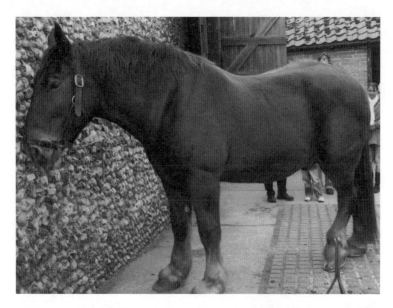

The horse was a symbol of fertility linked with the goddess Epona. Plough horses, such as this Suffolk Punch, (one of the oldest breeds of plough horse), helped to work the land and enable more crops to grow, thus the horse was intrinsically linked with the earth and the future prospects of a farming community.

ties to fertility made her the goddess of horse breeders and in Rome itself she was known as Regina, 'Queen'. The Roman influence carried Epona to many places as the patron deity of the Roman cavalry and she was known in Britain, carried on standards and even given her own feast day on 18 December. She was depicted now as an accomplished horse-woman, riding a fast steed with her cloak billowing behind her.

But Epona, though recognised in Britain, was also a Celtic French (Gaul) deity. She had a purely British counterpart, Rhiannon, who is known also as Great Queen 'Rigantona'. Rhiannon's story sees her transposed, not physically but by her actions, into a mount that must carry visitors to her husband's great hall. Her husband, Pwyll, met her whilst out riding. He saw a beautiful woman on a majestic horse ride by and desired to catch up with her and speak to her, but though he and his men rode swiftly after her and though her horse did not seemed to be running anymore speedily than them, they could not catch her. For two further days they chased her and still she kept out of reach, finally Pwyll called to her and she stopped and begged his help. Her father was intending to marry her to a man she disliked, Pwyll was so enchanted by her that he said he would marry her.

But before they were wed the old disliked suitor, Gwawl, tricked Pwyll into giving up Rhiannon. Fortunately she knew how to save the situation; she gave Pwyll a magic bag and sent him disguised as a beggar to the wedding feast. There he asked Gwawl to fill the bag with food, but no matter how much was put in, the bag grew larger and larger and could not be filled. Pwyll told Gwawl the only way to stop the bag expanding was for him to stand inside and shout 'enough'. Urged on by Rhiannon, Gwawl climbed into the bag. No sooner had he done so then Pwyll tied up the mouth of the sack and called his men, together they beat and kicked the helpless Gwawl. When they finally released him the battered Gwawl said he would leave and never return, leaving Pwyll and Rhiannon to marry in peace.

Already we can see Rhiannon has the makings of a goddess; like Epona she is first seen riding a horse so swiftly no one can catch up with it, then she is able to counteract Gwawl's trickery with her own magic and, as would be expected of a woman linked to an ancient fertility goddess, Rhiannon bore Pwyll a son. Then occurs a very bizarre part of the story that is never explained nor appears to have much logic. The child is stolen away one night. At apparently the same time a man named Teyrnon of Gwent was expecting his mare to foal. Every first of May she produced a fine colt, but as soon as it was born it vanished, so this year Teyrnon had brought her into his house so he could keep the foal. The mare as expected gave birth to a fine foal, but no sooner had it stood up when a giant clawed arm reached in through the window and started to drag away the foal by its mane. Teyrnon drew his sword and struck off the arm. A terrible wailing rose outside and Teyrnon rushed out to see what made the commotion, but he could not find the creature, yet when he returned to his door he found Rhiannon's son on the doorstep. He took the child in and fostered it.

This part of the story raises intriguing questions, why did the horse only give birth once a year and always on 1 May? Why was Rhiannon's son taken and why was the foal taken? And whose clawed arm reached through the window? If we consider Rhiannon a horse goddess once like Epona, in that originally she was depicted as a horse, could it be that Teyrnon's mare symbolises the goddess, could the mare and Rhiannon be the same creature, but still then why is the foal taken? Is it a sacrifice? Horses were often sacrificed to gods or for ritualistic purposes (see Chapter Four), therefore are the foal and Rhiannon's son emblems of this practice? Later the boy is given the saved colt to have as his own, thus further linking the two aspects of his mother as human and yet also as a horse. Clearly Rhiannon is deeply linked with horse cults; after it is discovered her son is missing her servant women accuse her of devouring the baby, Pwyll is not convinced but his son's mysterious disappearance is puzzling and he imposes a penance on his wife that she must wait at the gates everyday and carry visitors to the hall on her back like a horse.

Teyrnon heard of this and also of Rhiannon's missing son. He had once belonged to King Pwyll's retinue and as time went by he began to recognise the king in the boy and realised this must be Pwyll's lost son. Though it grieved him, for he had come to think of the boy as his own, he took the child to Pwyll's hall and there at the gates met Rhiannon sitting by the horse block. She told him to go no further that she must carry him, but Teyrnon showed her the boy and told her that it was her son. Overjoyed Rhiannon brought the boy before his father. Her penance was lifted, the boy was named Pryderi and later became a Celtic hero. Rhiannon is unmistakably a horse deity, her powers, her magic, her transposition into a horse, her ability to carry any who came to the gates and her son's later development into a great hero are all clues that she was once a goddess like Epona (if not Epona herself by a different name) and though later she became a mortal woman, though with supernatural gifts, it is more than likely she was once a deity of a cult, worshipped and loved for fertility. Her story is mysterious, parts are presumably missing having been lost in retelling or because they no longer meant anything to the people who listened, but what is left shows that once a horse goddess was worshipped in Britain or at least recognised, whether she was Epona renamed is difficult to say, yet the similarities are startling. Rhiannon is a magnificent and resourceful woman, her supernatural powers make her a mythical figure, but the trials of her life tied her to mortal women and her story enveloped her in the complex social issues of Celtic legend and storytelling.

HENGIST AND HORSA

In Bede's *Ecclesiastical History* he mentions the ill-fated King Vortigern who, being in danger of being overrun by the Picts, requests the help of two newly arrived Germanic strangers known as Hengist and Horsa. For Vortigern this was a disastrous decision; the two Saxon brothers had been forced to leave their homeland due to overpopulation and a lack of resources, Vortigern's invitation opened the door for them to set up a new kingdom in Britain. At first they assisted the king, helping him to drive back the Picts but Hengist realised that Vortigern was weak and easily manipulated. He sent for more Saxons to come to Britain and he encouraged the king to marry his daughter. This was a wily move as King Vortigern's sons from his first marriage protested against this new alliance. The eldest, Vortimer was proclaimed a rival sovereign and tried to drive the Saxons out of his country. His new stepmother swiftly quelled this rebellion by poisoning Vortimer and soon there was nothing stopping Hengist, who took control of large parts of England and forced Vortigern into retreat. The Saxons had settled in England and the Britons could not drive them out.

But were Hengist and Horsa real individuals or simply terms for a series of Saxon chieftains or even forgotten horse deities? Much of the earliest recorded history of this land is wrapped in myth and legend, even ancient historians who considered themselves to be writing accurate records of ancient events often documented mythological figures or episodes as factual happenings. Vortigern himself is linked with Arthurian legend; when he retreated from the Saxons he tried to build a hill fort to protect himself but no foundations could be successfully laid on the site he had chosen. His magicians told him he needed to find a boy who had no father and sacrifice him, whence the fort could be built. Messengers found such a boy, but when he was brought to the hill he was discovered to be a seer and told Vortigern that all his building problems were due to two dragons who lay beneath the hill, one red, one white. When the dragons were revealed they rose and fought each other. At first the white had the upper hand but then the red summoned its strength and succeeded in driving back its opponent. The boy explained that the white dragon symbolised the Saxons and the red symbolised the Britons, that eventually the Britons would triumph and drive out the Saxons but this would be too late for Vortigern and the king had no future. This boy's name was Merlin Ambrosius. So we can see that Vortigern was linked with one of the best known British legends, but what of his opponents?

It is fitting that the dragon symbolising the Saxons was white, as Hengist and Horsa's standards bore white horses, they are even linked, though rather tenuously, with the various white horses carved across England. They were supposedly of royal blood and descended from the Saxon god Woden (who is often muddled with Odin), though most Saxon kings claimed the god as their ancestor, but perhaps most interestingly their names mean Stallion (Hengist) and Horse (Horsa). This has lead to a suggestion that these brothers were not only linked to a horse cult, but also to a Germanic twin cult, mentioned by the Roman historian Tacitus. Evidence for either argument is scanty and while some books take Hengist and Horsa as historical fact others simply see them as mythological fiction. However, chroniclers like Bede readily assign dates and places to the Saxon brothers, giving a timeline for when they arrived in Britain and for Horsa's death. Aside from Hengist's daughter who married Vortigern, he had a son who went to fight the Irish. Perhaps Hengist and Horsa were in fact titles given to Saxon chieftains to symbolise their status and to link them to an ancient horse cult. There is really not enough evidence to draw a solid conclusion but what is clear is that the early chronicles of the first Saxons are a mixture of fact and fiction, whether Hengist and Horsa existed or not they were figureheads for the Saxons and their memory has lingered on long after their horse standards have fallen.

ODIN'S HORSE

When the Vikings reached the shores of Britain they brought with them their own religion separate from the old native Celtic gods and those of the previous invaders, the Anglo-Saxons (though the Germanic religion was not entirely dissimilar from the Norse philosophy). Paganism was still prevalent in Britain, though Christianity was rapidly spreading; the old and new faiths were intermingling, the Church turning pagan practices into Christian feast days and rituals (see Chapter Three). It is difficult to assess how widespread the invading Norsemen's religion was believed amongst native Britons, who had their own gods or God to worship, but certainly where the Vikings settled they believed in their old deities. Some of this belief must have spread to the Britons who lived near and traded with the Vikings, until the renewal of Christianity displaced the old faiths.

The horse in Norse mythology is a creature of power and magic. Often we only know of these wondrous steeds by their names and through the tasks their owners put them to, others are well known in the sagas and their creation is related in detail. The most famous of Norse stallions is the eight-legged Sleipnir who was ridden by Odin and was the best of all horses ever to live. Why he was eight-legged is a mystery, though interesting theories have been suggested – that his eight legs represent layers of worldly existence, or that he owes his extra legs to his master who was a death god and that he represents a coffin being carried, as four pall-bearers adds up to eight legs appearing beneath the coffin. Someone even laughingly suggested to me that perhaps a group of Vikings got very drunk (a frequent occurrence) and saw two horses standing so close together that it appeared there was one animal with eight legs. This currently seems to be as good a theory as any other and the mystery of Sleipnir's extra limbs remains unsolved.

Sleipnir's 'creation' is, however, much better recorded. The Norse gods, known collectively as the Aesir, had just finished establishing the realms of Midgard and Valhall when an anonymous builder approached them and offered to build a citadel in three seasons that would keep them secure from the ferocious giants. He asked as payment for this awesome project the fertility goddess Freyja and the sun and the moon. The Aesir agreed to this exchange only if the builder created the citadel in one season and was only helped by his stallion Svadilfari. The deal made, the builder began his work.

Odin's horse was named Sleipnir, a grey stallion of great strength and speed, who had eight legs, possibly due to an association with coffins and pall-bearers. Sleipnir's conception was due to the mischievous god Loki who transformed into a mare and seduced the stallion Svadilfari. (Author's own drawing)

Very swiftly it became clear the builder was making extraordinary progress, his stallion Svadilfari was able to carry large loads and had great powers of endurance. The Aesir became worried as they did not want to have to pay the builder and so Loki, the shape-shifting mischievous Norse god, was sent to delay the progress of the build. Loki transformed himself into a mare and lured away Svadilfari, the stallion caught up with Loki and mated with him. The builder's work was greatly hampered and he went into a rage when he could not finish the work on time and was killed by Thor. Loki had become pregnant by the stallion Svadilfari and eventually gave birth to Sleipnir. Odin took him to be his horse. But the underhanded behaviour of the gods that resulted in Sleipnir's creation, is strongly suggested in the *Voluspa*, a Viking saga, to be the beginning of the degeneration of the Aesir that will eventually lead to the Viking apocalypse, Ragnarok.

SKY AND SEA HORSES

Britain has a long tradition of mystical horses, whether they are linked to gods or are magical creatures in their own right, they roam the shores and meadows and not all of them would be a pleasure to meet. A large proportion of these spiritual equines seem to be linked to either the sky or water. There could be several reasons for this; sky horses tend to be associated with the passage of the sun and moon across the sky, and many ancient religions had gods who drove chariots that pulled the sun or moon over the world, it is a relatively logical way to explain why the sun constantly moves from dawn to dusk. Horses are chosen for this role, as opposed to other draught animals such as oxen, as they can pull objects far swifter and this was often necessary, for example in Norse mythology the sun is constantly being chased by a wolf (as is the moon) and therefore it must always be rushing across the sky to escape the creature's jaws.

The mythical figure at the centre of the Norse sun legends is Sol (Sun). She was the daughter of Mundilfari and was exceptionally beautiful, as was her brother Mani (Moon). Mundilfari betrothed Sol to a man called Glen. The gods were outraged apparently by the impertinence of the act and as punishment set Sol to drive the chariot of the sun and Mani to drive the chariot of the moon forever across the skies. Both were pursued by wolves who at the end of days, during the Ragnarok, would finally catch the hapless siblings and devour them.

Sol had two horses to drive her chariot, Arvak (Early Riser) and Alsvid (All-Swift). Arvak was said to have runes cut in his ear and Alsvid had them cut into his head. This may have been caused by confusion between Alsvid and a giant who had the same name and who possessed a great knowledge of runes. In another version of the sun legend a giant called Day was given a chariot and horses by the gods and set to the task of driving them round the earth once every twenty-four hours. One of Day's horses was called Shining Mane and it was said he lit up the world with the radiant light that shone from his mane.

Other Norse gods also possessed fabulous horses; the watchman Heimdall owned the steed Gulltopr or Gulltopp (either translated as Golden Mare or Golden Top), which some suggest links him to sun gods and sun horses in classical mythology, perhaps because he is the watchman who will signal to the Aesir the coming of Ragnarok. He may have once held more importance as the central figure of a cult but even by the thirteenth century when his legends were being written down he had become obscure.

Sea or water horses tend to be of a nastier variety than their sky horse counterparts. Legends say that white water horses come out of the sea fully bridled and saddled to graze on nearby pastures, but anyone foolish enough to mount one is instantly dragged into the sea and drowned. Is this an allusion to the dangerous nature of the

Valkyrie and Horse. The Valkyries flew down to battlefields on magnificent horses to carry off the dead to the great halls of Valhalla, where feasting and fighting were the main activities. This nineteenth-century print shows the typical Victorian idea of these female angels of death.

ocean? Perhaps it is the roaring of the waves that could be supposed to sound like a large herd of horses stampeding that made people imagine horses existed in the water. These are tentative suppositions with little evidence to make them sound convincing, but it is certain that the Celts believed in sea horses, after all the sea god Manannan Mac Lir had glistening sea horses, among many other wonders, in his domain and was said to ride the horse Splendid Mane.

Yet, in the main, horses that rose from the water were not to be trusted and should be avoided at all costs. The most famous of these dangerous equines is the Scottish Kelpie, which was in fact a water sprite that often took the form of a horse to lure travellers into riding it, whereupon it would toss them into the water and devour them. There was also a Neugle in Shetland akin to the Kelpie that would drown anyone foolish enough to try and ride it. It was said to be a sure sign that a person would drown if they saw a kelpie grazing by a lake or river and this fabled creature has many legends attached to it. In Aberdeen, legend has it that a man was hurrying home to his sick wife and needed to cross the River Don. Finding the bridge swept away he rather recklessly accepted a Kelpie's offer to ferry him across. They were barely halfway there when the Kelpie submerged and tried to drown its unfortunate rider. Somehow the man managed to escape its clutches and swim to the other side. As he raced away the furious Kelpie hurled a boulder at him which became known as The Kelpie's Boulder.

Another legend tells of how a Kelpie was defeated by another fairy creature, a Water Bull. In itself the Water Bull was dangerous as it was said to mingle with a normal herd and then lead them all into the water of a loch or river so they might become part of the fairy

Horses seem intrinsically linked with water, from the white water horses who would graze fully saddled on pastures near the sea, only to vanish back into the water if anyone tried to mount them, to the fiendish kelpies, half man, half horse who were viewed as an omen of drowning if found grazing near a river. (Early twentieth-century postcard 'After the Day's Work')

herds. Legend has it that a wealthy Scottish farmer found such a calf amongst his herd, it was strangely marked and its ears were oddly shaped. He asked the advice of a wise woman who said that it must be shut in a house by itself and only fed on the milk of three cows. The calf grew to a huge size in a matter of days and frightened the farmer by throwing itself at the door of its prison, but the farmer dare not let it out.

Then, some weeks later, a lone servant girl went out to tend the cattle that were grazing by a loch. The day was warm and she fell asleep on the bank, but not for long as she heard a noise and opened her eyes. A man in grand clothes was approaching her, yet despite his fancy appearance his hair was in a tangled mess, clumped and hanging in tails. He stopped before the girl and requested that she might tidy his hair. Reluctant, but frightened to refuse, the girl agreed. The stranger laid his head in her lap and she began pulling apart his terribly knotted hair, which she soon discovered was tangled with a slimy water weed from the loch. The man's clothes also had the smell of the water and with a pang of horror the girl realised she was dealing with a Kelpie and not a real man. She kept quiet, afraid the Kelpie would drag her into the water if she screamed or cried for help. Fortunately the creature fell asleep as she untangled its hair and shortly it seemed to be deeply dozing. Cautiously she untied her apron and lowered the Kelpie's head to the ground as she started to move away.

She began to run with all her heart but the Kelpie woke and transformed itself into a horse, before charging after her. The girl screamed and the wise woman heard the commotion and came to the door of her house. Seeing the Kelpie she told the girl to race to the farm and release the Water Bull. The girl did as she was told and though she was fearful of the Water Bull, she was far more terrified of the Kelpie and she wrenched back the bolt of the Water Bull's house and sprang to one side. The Water Bull came crashing out, the first thing it saw was the Kelpie racing towards the farm and it set its head down and charged towards the beast. Horse and bull crashed together and a terrible fight ensued, they spun and struck at each other moving faster and faster until they were nothing more than a blur on the landscape as they whirled and fought. They eventually came to the loch and, still fighting, dived beneath the icy waters.

Some days later the Water Bull's body was washed ashore horribly wounded and torn. When the sun's first light rested upon it, the body turned to dust. But despite the Water Bull's death the Kelpie never returned and the cattle herds could be tended without fear.

Whatever we make of the horse deities of the past we cannot deny that they were deeply important to our ancestors, they pulled the sun and moon, they predicted death, they represented fertility, they could even be a creature of magic and danger, but they were also a symbol of the future and hope. As long as the horses pulled the sun across the sky, so a new day would come, and as long as there were fertility goddesses like Epona new life would be created, and when the end inevitably came, so too there were those final ethereal horses who would take the dead to their last resting place. And so the horse was part of every stage of life from birth to death, from beginning to end, it only made sense to honour such a creature so closely intertwined with the cruel and yet wonderful, mortal existence.

THREE

CHRISTIAN HORSE SYMBOLISM

THE HORSE IN THE BIBLE

For the Vikings, ancient Celts and Romans the horse had been a divine creature, a god or godly symbol. Christianity did not take this view; other than the unicorn which could symbolise Christ's purity, the horse was a practical animal that was used significantly in war throughout the Bible. Though not all Biblical cultures used the horse, many valued their equines mainly for pulling war chariots or for cavalry units. Egypt was an important source of horses. The Bible records that the Hebrews were banned from amassing horses, they themselves had been chased by chariots and cavalry when fleeing Egypt and were now warned by God not to, 'make the people return to Egypt to get more of them [horses], for the Lord has told you, "You are not to go back that way again".' (Deut. 17:16).

The first horseman of the Apocalypse rode a white steed and carried a bow, he is, 'a conqueror bent on conquest' (Rev. 5:6). This white horseman in Norwich Cathedral is being disgorged by a monster or demon, perhaps representing the jaws of Hell. (Used by permission of the Chapter of Norwich Cathedral)

The second rider has a fiery red horse, which springs forth when the seal is broken. This horseman is given the power to take peace from the earth and incite men to war. (Used by permission of the Chapter of Norwich Cathedral)

The third horseman rides a black horse and carries a pair of scales. Black horses are also commonly associated with the Devil. Medieval stories often talk of riders on black horses coming to funerals to snatch the souls of the wicked, or chasing the spirit of a sinful person, catching them just before they make it to the sanctuary of a church. (Used by permission of the Chapter of Norwich Cathedral)

The last horseman rode a pale, sickly horse, his name is death and he joins his brothers to torment the world. The horse in this carving looks quite healthy and sprightly to be death's horse. (Used by permission of the Chapter of Norwich Cathedral)

This command was eventually ignored by the Hebrew King David who, after defeating Hadadezer, son of the king of Zobah, regained control of the land along the Euphrates river and, 'captured a thousand of his chariots, seven thousand charioteers and twenty thousand foot soldiers. He hamstrung all but a hundred of the chariot horses.' (II Sam. 8:4). This disobedience was rewarded by an uprising by David's son Abasalom, which was quelled, fortunately for David, only for twelve years later his son Adonijah to do exactly the same. But Adonijah was not destined to be king. David was told of the plot and had his son Solomon hastily crowned as his successor. Adonijah had to swear allegiance to his brother and give up his only plans of gaining the throne. All this due to horses, on both occasions when Absalom and Adonijah prepared to usurp their father they gathered chariots and horses, along with fifty men to run ahead of them. In the Old Testament the horse was a status symbol of kings, it donated power and military strength, but the horse in the New Testament was a much different creature, one that could be feared.

Horses and chariots were used both in God's armies and in the armies of his enemy, the fallen angel Satan. In the Book of Revelations, where the Apocalypse is described it is God who unleashes a dreadful assortment of monstrous horses and riders on the world to cleanse it before the Kingdom of Christ can be formed. Many bizarre creations are summoned at the Last Judgement including creatures with six wings and eyes covering their entire bodies, but the horse makes a prominent appearance showing its importance in the Biblical world, particularly as the steeds of the Four Horsemen of the Apocalypse. To begin the Apocalypse and to purge the world of sinners seven seals must be broken. Only one being is worthy enough to break the seals, a lamb, 'looking as if it had been slain' (Rev. 5:6), which comes forth and breaks the seals each in turn. The first seal releases a white horse, its rider carries a bow and is given a crown, he is, 'a conqueror bent on conquest'. (Rev. 6:2).

The second seal is broken and this time a fiery red horse bursts forth, its rider is given the power to take peace from the earth and turn men against each other in war. He carries a sword. The third seal reveals a black horse and a rider who holds a pair of scales and the last brings forth a pale horse, whose rider's name is Death. So these are the horsemen who will bring war, famine, plague and finally death to the world, and they ride their respectively coloured horses.

But more is to come, after the seventh seal is broken there come seven angels with trumpets and various natural disasters occur as each blows his trumpet, mainly earthquakes and the world being ravaged by fire. When the fifth angel blows his trumpet a swarm of terrible locusts is set on the world to torment men for five months they, 'looked like horses prepared for battle' (Rev. 9:7), they wore crowns of gold had human faces and hair, teeth like a lion's, breastplates of iron and stings in their tails. 'The sound of their wings was like the thundering of many horses and chariots rushing into battle.'

The sixth angel blows his trumpet and four angels that have been bound at the great river Euphrates are released and they take forth two-hundred million mounted troops to kill a third of mankind. These horses and riders have breastplates fiery red, dark blue and yellow as sulphur. The heads of the horses resembled lions and they spewed fire, smoke and sulphur from their mouths, their tails were like snakes with their own heads with which they could strike and kill. 'A third of mankind was killed by the three plagues of fire, smoke and sulphur that came out of their mouths'. (Rev. 9:18).

There is one final horseman who comes to defeat Satan. He appears on a white horse and is called Faithful and True. He is to ride out to judge and make war, 'His eyes are like blazing fire, and on his head are many crowns. He has a name written on him that no-one knows but he himself. He is dressed in a robe dipped in blood, and his name is the Word of God' (Rev. 19:12). This rider, with the armies of heaven on white horses and in white linen following him must fight the Devil himself along with his armies and defeat him. On his thigh is written King of Kings and Lord of Lords and from his mouth strikes a sharp sword with which he can strike down nations.

But why is there an Apocalypse at all which causes such devastation to the world? The answer is that at the time when Revelations was written Christianity was being constantly attacked and undermined by other forms of worship, faithful Christians were being persecuted and could see no end to their suffering. Revelations is promising God's children that they will be rewarded if they remain faithful, these fearsome armies will cull the sinners and loyal Christians will be welcomed into a New Jerusalem. But first many battles had to be won and for that purpose the horse was required, particularly in the last battle against Satan. It is interesting to wonder whether the historical image of heroic knights on white horses stems from the final images of the heavenly armies riding white steeds. After all, the Devil is portrayed in Revelations as a dragon and there was a very famous knightly saint who rode a white charger and slew a dragon. St George, however, did not herald the beginning of a new age, though it is curious how white knights and white chargers are integrally linked with our ideas of salvation, how many stories both medieval and later focus on such iconography, after all white symbolises purity. It seems the plethora of legends surrounding the horse have much to owe to the books of the Bible.

SAINTLY HORSES

Early saints seem integrally linked with animals, probably because for most of our existence, humankind has been dependant on the animal world for its very survival. Saints had an affinity with animals, sometimes criticising the people around them for not being so attuned to the world as animals were. St Francis of Assisi famously talked to birds and chastised a wolf for terrorising a village, after which it never caused trouble again. Saints were protectors of both people and animals. It is hardly surprising then that wax pilgrimage figures were found in Exeter cathedral after bomb damage required the building to be repaired in 1943, amongst the wax figures, was part of a horse's head. The odd collection of wax effigies which were discovered in a cavity on top of the stone screen surrounding the choir, usually only represented the part of the body that was causing the person's or animal's illness, . They are thought to have been originally laid on the tomb of Bishop Edmund Lacy. The Bishop died in 1455 and was considered so saintly in life that in death it was believed that his tomb held healing properties and pilgrims would travel to the cathedral to lay their offerings on the grave and pray for their own or their animal's ailments to be healed. The horse's head presumably represented an animal that was ill and its owner had travelled specifically to the tomb to pray for his horse to be healed. Unfortunately we will never know if it was successful.

Saints were often portrayed with their horses. This carving on a thirteenth-century chest could represent St George, with his shield bearing the English cross and his lance spearing an odd animal difficult to identify, possibly a deer.

Bishop Lacy was not alone in acquiring healing powers after his death. Many saints have similar claims, sometimes it is not their tombs that become places of pilgrimage, wells blessed by saints are often considered to have healing properties in their water and even the site of a saint's martyrdom can become a shrine.

However, sometimes the connection between saint and site is unclear. At Ippolitts in Hertfordshire, one tradition claims the Roman saint Hippolytus, is buried beneath the church altar. Hippolytus was supposed to be a famous martyr torn apart by horses. This unpleasant fate – shared by several saints including Anastasius and Quirinus – caused him to be associated, at least in Hertfordshire, with the ability to heal sick horses. Unfortunately, it is very unlikely that the saint was buried in Britain, as it is recorded that St Hippolytus on his death was brought back to Rome and buried in the cemetery at Via Tiburtina. It is believed that it was his tomb that was unearthed during excavations in 1882. Ippolitts (the name itself is a derivative of Hippolytus) church is dedicated to St Hippolytus and in times past sick horses were taken in through the north door of the church and led to the altar where the priest would touch them with the relics of the saint in return for an offering.

Sadly St Hippolytus appears to have very little connection to horses. Original thinking was that he had indeed been martyred for becoming an Antipope – heading a separate church due to his disagreement with the elected pope over his interpretation of Christianity – by being torn apart by wild horses. In truth Hippolytus was exiled to the island of Sardinia around AD 235, where he died. The idea that he was gruesomely martyred appears to stem from a confusion over names. There was another Hippolytus, son of the Greek Theseus, who is not connected to the church but who was killed when his horses bolted and, depending on the source, either tore him apart or dragged him to his death. He was a renowned horseman and it seems that at some point his name and the name of St Hippolytus were confused and so the legend of a martyred saint who could heal sick and injured horses arose.

ST PATRICK

St Patrick is tied in two ways with the mythology of the horse; not only was he reputed to own a magical steed, but he met and converted some of the pagan heroes of the old Celtic tradition. He first came to Ireland as a British slave captured by the Celts. He escaped aged seventeen and fled back to Britain where he trained as a monk before eventually returning to Ireland to convert the people to Christianity. Patrick became the patron saint of Ireland and many legends have circulated about him. It was reputed that his horse had the capacity to carry great loads and that it had once saved his life when a sea monster was hunting him. The horse jumped straight up a cliff face escaping its pursuer. Where its feet touched the ground after this extraordinary jump a well sprang into life and it was said later that such a well had magical properties.

Patrick's associations with horses were not always so pleasant; legend has it that he drove his chariot three times over his sister Lupita or Lupait, because he was enraged that she had succumbed to the sin of lust and had fallen pregnant. Happily, this is unlikely to be true. The site where she is buried in Armagh was once a piece of land known as the Graves or the Church of the Relics. Patrick had requested a piece of high ground called the Ridge of the Willows from King Daire, to use for the exercise of his religion. Daire however gave him a piece of lower ground, the Graves, and then proceeded to allow his groom to graze a fine horse there. Patrick was outraged that the king would allow beasts to trample sacred ground and told the groom to remove the horse. The groom ignored Patrick and left the horse on the land overnight, when he returned in the morning, the horse lay dead. King Daire was infuriated, he sent his executioners to slay Patrick, but before they arrived Daire suffered a stroke and fell dead. Finally his wife stepped in and seeing things had got out-of-hand, called back the executioners and begged Patrick to restore both horse and husband. Patrick relented and sent holy water back to the queen. Once sprinkled over man and beast they both came back to life. It seems that this incident, among others, finally convinced King Daire that it was best to let Patrick have the piece of land – the saint seemed to have a way of getting things he wanted.

Patrick, better than many saints, demonstrates the transition from paganism to Christianity. Though it is suggested he is in fact the Celtic god Lugh Christianised, the truth is that Patrick is too much of a historical figure to be an incarnation of an ancient god. But there are strange stories of Patrick associating with figures from Celtic mythology that show that the Irish could not give up their old gods easily. Perhaps one of the saddest tales is Patrick's meeting with the Celtic hero and poet Oisin. Oisin had a supernatural birth, his mother had been transformed into a deer by a shaman and only gave birth to a human son because she did not lick him when he was born. He became a great poet and roamed with the Fianna, a war-band, and saw many battles with them before he left to visit the Otherworld, Tir na nOg. There he lived with his wife, the beautiful Niamh, for three years until he started to long for his home and wished to see Ireland one last time. Reluctantly Niamh agreed he could go and gave him a white horse who knew the way back to Ireland, but she warned him that if ever he was to dismount from the horse and set foot on Irish soil he would never be able to return to Tir na nOg and would never see her again. Oisin took her warning and returned on the horse to Ireland, but as he rode across the countryside he found his home greatly altered. Talking to local inhabitants he discovered he had been gone for three centuries and the Fianna had long since died out.

It was only by accident that Oisin finally set foot on Irish soil. He was helping some men move a rock out of the road and the saddle girth snapped and in struggling to not slip off the horse, Oisin put his feet on the ground. Instantly the white horse turned and raced back to Tir na nOg, leaving Oisin in Ireland, his youthful body rapidly aging and becoming a withered old man. It was at this point that Patrick heard of him and went to meet him. He listened to the old man's stories of the Fianna and of his sad return to Ireland to discover it greatly changed. Lastly Patrick spoke to him of Christianity and Oisin agreed to be baptised. As the ceremony ended, Oisin, still sitting at the roadside where he had first stood on Irish ground, died peacefully.

Oisin was not the only hero to return from the timeless land of Tir na nOg, nor was he the only one who forgot the warnings to remain on the magical white horse and set foot on Irish ground. St Patrick also seems adept at meeting these unfortunate heroes. The Celtic hero Ushen was tricked into stepping off his horse when he tried to help an old woman who was struggling with her load of turf. As in the case of Oisin as the white horse returns to its own land so Ushen is left in Ireland aging rapidly. Patrick comes across him dying and tries to tell him of heaven and God but Ushen is not interested, which greatly sorrows Patrick, so he offers to grant the dying hero's wishes. Ushen first wishes to be buried in a special place, Slew Gullion, up high with stones over him, which Patrick agrees to, and then, because Patrick has made mention of a bull that is constantly destroying anything he builds, Ushen wishes for the strength to defeat this bull. So Patrick does as he asks and gives Ushen one last drop of strength. Ushen goes down to face the bull and when he finds it he strikes it on the head and it dies. Later Patrick goes to find the hero and discovers him curled up in the skin of the dead bull. Patrick shows great sadness at Ushen's death and buries him as requested up high on Slew Gullion.

What the legends of St Patrick seem to show us is that the Celts even as they came to accept Christianity could not forgot their old pagan heroes. They could not simply ignore them and consign them to history, rather they took the unusual step of converting them also to Christianity. So the pagan heroes became Christian converts and who better to transform them than Ireland's own magical patron saint?

ST COLUMBA

Columba, like St Patrick, is linked to Celtic mythology in particular to Celtic heroes, though this time it is because Columba may have been looked upon as ranking with or being one of those heroes. Columba was also a member of the ruling dynasty of Donegal, giving him royal blood. He was born AD 521 and was educated at St Finian's at Molville, being ordained as a monk around AD 546. In AD 561 he is said to have prayed for his kinsmen to be successful in battle, which resulted in him being the subject of a censure orchestrated by the Meaths, political opponent's of his family. He left Ireland in

AD 563 and travelled to Scotland where King Conall of Dalraida gave him the island of Iona where Columba founded a monastery and eventually died in AD 597.

Columba knew he was dying and told his followers that he would soon part from them. As his last days approached he visited those working on the far side of the island to tell them he was to depart this life soon. A few days after, whilst giving mass, Columba had a vision of an angel and a week later he visited the nearby barn to bless it and the corn that lay inside. It was as he was returning from the barn with his servant Diarmaid that the strange phenomena of the old white horse occurred. Columba needed to rest and sat at the roadside. Shortly a horse approached him, it was the animal used to carry milk-pails to the monastery. It came close to the saint and pressed its head into his chest and as it did so it began to weep tears and foam at the mouth, whinnying pitifully. Diarmaid would have driven it away but Columba would not let him, remarking that though Diarmaid could only know of the saint's departure through being told of it, the horse must have been told by God himself, for else it could not have known its master was dying. He blessed the horse and it turned away. Not long after Columba died.

Some speculate that this incident links Columba to the Celtic heroes of old. The horse's mystical ability to foresee its master's death is similar to Cuchulain's grey horse that wept bloody tears when it predicted his death. The horse is strongly linked to Celtic nobility, Celtic kings were 'married' to mares and burying favoured steeds with their noble masters was commonly practiced at wealthy funerals. Like Patrick before him, Columba bridged the gap between the old Celtic religion and the newer religion of Christianity, he was a saint who became immortalised through heroic deeds equal to those of his mythological counterparts. Nevertheless, he was still a saint and his horse did not predict his death, it was informed by God. Not Cuchulain then, not a Celtic hero, but Columba, a Christian saint.

ST ALDHELM

St Aldhelm was born around AD 640, descended from the Wessex nobility and connected with the royal court. He became abbot of Malmesbury, though the date of his appointment is uncertain. William of Malmesbury writing about the saint several centuries later gives the date as AD 675, but it is uncertain if this is correct. Aldhelm was a great writer and church builder, he also was said to have given a bell to the Abbey, which had the power to quell a storm when it was rung. This magical bell perhaps caused concern to the pope who, local legend has it, summoned Aldhelm. The saint had but two days notice and knew he had to make haste. He drew a chalk circle on the floor and called for a fleet spirit to take him to Rome.

The first spirit to appear was asked how swift it was and it answered as fleet as a bird in the air. It was turned away and a second spirit summoned, again Aldhelm put forth the question and the spirit replied as fleet as an arrow out of a bow. That was not good enough either. Aldhelm summoned a third spirit, this one appeared as a flame and when asked the question answered as fleet as thought. Finally the saint was satisfied and commanded that the spirit should turn itself into a horse which he could ride. This is what it immediately did, some say it changed into a winged white horse, others that it transformed into a black steed, either way a saddle was placed upon its back and Aldhelm mounted it.

The horse flew him swiftly to Rome and he landed in the stable yard, where the groom came forth and asked him (apparently unfazed by flying horses) what Aldhelm's steed might eat. The saint promptly replied that he would eat a peck of live coals. Aldhelm then went to meet the pope. The legend does not relate what happens at the meeting, but presumably all went well for nine days later Aldhelm collected his horse and it flew him home again.

This is a very old tale, at least going back to the seventeenth century and is told not just of Aldhelm, but of St Mungo (also known as Kentigern) and more notorious characters such as Faustus and Francis Drake. The tale is certainly not one that a saint would probably like to be associated with considering its elements of witchcraft and magic. After all, what is Aldhelm summoning? They are called spirits but seem to behave like demons; they are summoned in a chalk circle synonymous with spell casting, transform their shape and eat live coals! Is it likely that a spirit of God would do such things? It is doubtful, as it is also doubtful that the legend goes back to Aldhelm's time, some historical sources even omit Aldhelm's supposed trip to Rome. More likely the legend circulated at a later date, though for what purpose is unclear, though many saints do own magical horses in local folklore, perhaps the story has become confused with some other person like the legend of St Hippolytus. What is clear is that the horse is as important in Christianity as it was to the pagan religions that came before it. It was not worshipped, nor was it deified, it was not a sacred animal, but it was a creature of domestic importance whether this was because of war or simply, like

Columba's old nag, it carried milk-pails. The horse was still a creature of magic and the early saints coming into a world still engulfed in stories of superhuman heroes and timeless realms found themselves being transposed into those worlds, albeit in a Christian form. Times were changing, but the old ways still lingered – the horse was still a magical creature whether it belonged to the hero Cuchulain or St Patrick. The religion had changed but the horse was still needed to plough the fields, pull the carts and to be the status symbol of kings, that part of life had not changed. The Celtic heroes had given way to the Christian saints, but the horse was still there, still vitally important to the people, still veiled in a wealth of superstition and folklore. Nothing could change that.

FOUR

HORSE SACRIFICES AND BURIALS

The sacrificing and ritual burial of animals is an ancient custom: a Neanderthal grave from Skhul cave; Mount Carmel contained a man with the jaws of a wild boar clutched in his arms; Bronze Age tombs in Jericho have revealed warrior graves containing asses; and other sites have contained horses buried presumably beside their masters. This custom seems to have been practice across most of the ancient world and great numbers of horse burials have been found in Britain. Of 2000 cremations discovered at Spong Hill, Norfolk, forty-six per cent contained animal remains, horses being the most frequent find. Similar discoveries of animal sacrifice have been unearthed at other early cremation sites such as Millgate, Newark-on-Trent, and Illington, Norfolk. The purpose behind many of the animal offerings was to provide the deceased with food for their journey to the afterlife. Sheep, pig and cattle bones tend to be found as only parts of the animal, as though they were placed in the grave as joints of meat.

However horses were generally not considered a food animal, in fact eating their meat, except on ritual occasions such as the coronation of an Irish king, was considered taboo. Horses were buried in graves to serve their masters in the next life, therefore they are mainly found in warrior graves though there are other examples, which suggest the horse was used for an agricultural purpose before its death. In some cases, the sacrifice of the animal may have had totemic elements, the horse may have been representational of a deity such as Epona, but once in the ground it is difficult to know what the ritualistic purpose of the horse's death was. Fragmentary accounts of funeral practices from ancient scholars tell us only so much, and though archaeology allows us to make some scientific deductions, we may never fully understand just what role horses played in the burials of our ancestors.

FUNERAL RITES

The practice of mourning the dead seems to be a distinctly human custom, the elaborate means to which cultures go to ensure their dead loved ones pass peacefully into the next life are as diverse as they are bizarre. Funerals have been in existence since the earliest times of modern human beings; Neolithic barrows show that care was taken in the burial of important members of society. At a chambered barrow in Notgrave, Somerset, horse remains were found along with the bones of ox and pig, perhaps the horse was a tamed animal or perhaps it was hunted for its meat, either way it was considered an animal worthy to be buried in the barrow. Similarly at Handley,

Dorset, horse bones and reindeer antler fragments were found in a barrow along with a human inhumation. But evidence for what the animals signified, how they were sacrificed and who the person they were buried with was is scanty.

Similarly in the Bronze Age, horse remains in graves tell us little of why the animal was sacrificed, except in cases such as Mold, Flintshire, where a chieftain was accompanied to the afterlife by his horse, its gold-plated peytrel the only remnant of the animal, its bones having disintegrated. Throughout the Iron Age horses were placed in the graves of notable individuals, sometimes there is only a skeleton, other times a chariot is included and the animal's trappings. Yet as history moves on written sources begin to give us a glimpse into the ancient burials rites of our ancestors. Often this is all the evidence we have for these practices as chants and rituals, unless written down, are not recorded in archaeological sources, we are reliant on contemporary historians to give us an idea of just what was happening at these funerals.

Roman Burials
In the Greek *Iliad* the funeral rites of Patroclus included funeral pyres and leading horses three times round the body, just some of the elaborate rituals that accompanied a grand funeral. The Romans were no different to their Greek counterparts in their desire to honour the noble dead with dancing, games, music, fire, mourners and human and animal sacrifices. Chambers have been excavated that show lavish funerals involving feasting and fire. An example of this rite was found at Folly Lane, St Albans and there is another example at Cambridge. In these rituals the deceased was laid out in the

chamber over which stood a timber shrine. Feasting was carried out and items probably belonging to the deceased were placed within the chamber, including gaming pieces, flagons of wine, glass vessels, and a flute. Animals were sacrificed, amongst them horses and then the body was cremated and buried separately. At the Cambridge site the timber shrine was also set on fire and the burnt remains collapsed into the chamber along with the remnants of feasting and sacrifice.

This ritual destruction was carried out in the mid-second century and was possibly linked to earlier rites of the Iron Age. The animals were sacrificed to please the gods, perhaps to ensure the deceased found his way to the afterlife. An intaglio found on the site bore the image of Bacchus, a god of wine, feasting and general over-indulgence. The Romans had also adopted the Celtic Epona into their religion and perhaps she was thought of as the horse was led to its slaughter.

Anglo Saxon Burials (Pagan)

The Scandinavian practices of burying the dead entered England with the Anglo Saxons, and there are many good examples of their customs represented in the eastern counties at sites such as Sutton Hoo and Lakenheath. Saxons could be inhumed or cremated, in either case animal bones are often discovered with them. However, not all finds indicate sacrificial offerings, horse teeth are often found in cremations and burials, but these represent gaming pieces. Such teeth are usually filed flat on the top to make them sit better on a board and some are stained to denote a different player's pieces. But horse sacrifices are found; at Sutton Hoo five burials contained horses, at other sites it appears animals were cremated whole, but the majority of graves that

This photograph shows some of the burial mounds at Sutton Hoo. For a time this was a royal cemetery and beneath the tree on the right the bones of a prince and his horse were found buried in separate graves. The mounds have significantly shrunk since their first creation; originally they would have been much higher and would have stood out boldly in the landscape to mark the final resting place of kings.

contain horse bones usually only contain parts, either a skull or leg bones or even just the harness. This was more economical (burying just the harness spares a healthy animal and means it can still be used), as was the occasional custom of burying an old or lame horse with the body.

The horse held great significance for the Anglo Saxons. It was used for racing, warfare, agriculture and it was a status symbol. Eating horse flesh was taboo to them, but when a nobleman died it was his horse who accompanied him to the grave, so that he might ride his steed in the next life. The burial of grave goods came to an end with the conversion to Christianity of the Anglo Saxons, as did by and large the sacrifice of horses to honour the dead.

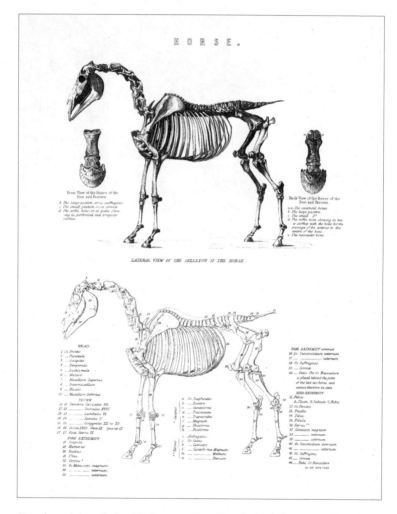

Horse bones are usually found in fragments. Generally, only the skull or a part of the leg bone is buried, but occasionally whole skeletons are found intact. These burials are usually part of a ritual sacrifice performed at a funeral, though on other occasions the reason for the burial is a mystery. (Horse print, c. 1880)

Viking Burials

In pre-Christian Sweden, at the Old Uppsala temple it was common practice even into the eleventh century for sacrifices to be offered every nine years. When the sacrifice was due nine male examples of every living thing were killed, this included men, and their blood was used to placate the gods. The bodies of the victims were hung in a scared grove and dogs and horses hung beside human sacrifices. To Vikings the blood of a sacrifice was of utmost importance, it was sprinkled over altars and around temples, because it represented a living being's life force and so it was the blood of the victims the gods would most want.

When the Vikings came to Britain their violent funeral practices did not stop. They buried their dead in ships, some vessels being buried beneath mounds, others were set alight, just like that of the god Balder. His funeral pyre was set on a ship along with his wife and horse. Many British Viking grave goods include horses, along with other everyday items. The Vikings associated horses with Odin and his horse Sleipnir. Odin used Sleipnir to travel between the mortal world and Asgard, the realm of the gods. He was a god of death as well as war, so it is unsurprising that horses were sacrificed in his name and buried with warriors, after all in Valhalla, the warrior's afterlife, there was to be much warring and a man would need his horse along with his weapons. Other animals sacrificed at the burials are thought to signify different gods.

Medieval Burials

Christianity stopped the practice of animal sacrifice to pagan deities, but relics of it remained. Figurines representing animals might be placed in a grave or offered at pilgrimage sites. At Henry V's funeral four horses pulled his coffin up the nave of Westminster. They were then given, along with their bridles to the lord abbot. In some ways this still represented a sacrifice; the animals were not slaughtered but given to the Church in return for prayers to help the deceased's soul out of purgatory and into heaven. Other objects, money and even land were given in a similar manner, though they were usually ostensibly said to be for forgotten tithes. The result of handing over horses and other items was that the Church owned things that would have previously ended up in the ground and been useless to them. For assisting a person's soul the Church earned possessions and wealth, for the deceased they were guaranteeing a speedy entry into heaven, something that their pagan predecessors equally desired. In both cases they sacrificed some of their belongings and animals, one for blood the other for prayer.

A WARRIOR'S GRAVE

Whilst a general overview of horse burial practices gives us an idea of the animal's significance to our ancestors, often much more than just this can be unearthed along with the bones. Sometimes strange rituals become evident, while, at other times the obvious care taken of the animal is apparent.

A poignant burial was excavated close to the river Thames in 2002. The site was a Roman burial ground of the late second to fourth century. The bones of a man were found in one grave, a horse's skull was laid between his knees. The skull had lost its lower

jaw suggesting that the animal had died naturally some time before
the man and that the head had been kept out of the ground long
enough for the flesh and muscles to disintegrate and the jaw to be
lost. Possibly it was placed on a stake. Eventually when the man died
the skull was buried with him. Could it be that the horse was a
much loved animal? A farming animal or a riding horse? When
it died what drove its owners to retain its skull, did they know
the man was dying and wanted to bury him with his horse? We
cannot answer these questions, but it does seem that this was a
cherished animal that despite its death before its master its skull
was kept so that they could be reunited in a grave and perhaps in
the afterlife.

A stranger burial has been uncovered during excavations at
Nosterfield Quarry, North Yorkshire. Work has been going on at
this site since 1995 and the archaeological evidence being uncovered
spans a rich wealth of early British history. An unusual burial pit
containing four horses was found in December 2003, the grave
may date to the Iron Age as the landscape around includes many
prehistoric features. What is unusual about this grave is that it seems
to have contained no human remains, only four complete horse
skeletons. The bones were not buried deep enough for the top layer
to avoid the damaging effects of centuries of ploughing, but the
lower skeletons gave an insight into a strange ritual. The skeletons
were buried in pairs stacked on top of each other. The lower pair
were buried on their right sides, back to back, their heads touching
each other's tail. From what remains of the upper pair of horses it is
though they were buried on their left sides, in a reverse of the lower
pair, very little of the upper bones remained.

Skeletons can tell us a remarkable amount about the living animal or person. The lower horses were only the size of a small pony, one being smaller than the other. They seem to have both been male, about seven years old, animals in the prime of their life. They were working animals as evidence of arthritis in the spine indicates stress and strain on the horses' backs, one was suffering from a condition known as spavin where the lower bones of the leg become partially fused, the result would have been a lame animal. The bones of the upper skeletons were too disjointed and fragmentary to tell much about these animals, though their apparent smaller size and lack of canine teeth could possibly suggest they were female.

These animals appear to have been a ritual sacrifice, for what reason is impossible to tell. Perhaps other animals were sick and a sacrifice of four valuable horses, one lame, was thought to placate the god causing the illness. Perhaps they were sacrificed to aid fertility of both animals and people, or to prevent a famine or other natural disaster. There is no way at the present time of knowing. All we can say is that during an early period of history in North Yorkshire four working horses in their prime were led to a grave, killed and buried in elaborate positions atop one another. Their ritual significance to their tribe was as important as their working ability, a significance we have lost or forgotten.

Saxon burials reveal how the horse and its harness had developed and changed since the earlier burials mentioned above. Most Saxon horses were also no bigger than ponies only measuring around fourteen hands, they were probably quite stocky and well built, suited to a damp and wet climate. When being ridden they had no saddles, but did wear bridles, two of these bridles with their fittings have been found, one at the famous Sutton Hoo burial ground and another at the Lakenheath military base, Suffolk, where a sizable Saxon cemetery has been found under the foundations of the air base. The bridles were made to individual taste and were of intricate design gilded with gold and silver inlays. The Sutton Hoo horse had human figure designs on the metal strap ends of its harness, a reverse of the habit for Saxon belts to have animal designs at the end of their straps. The Sutton Hoo horse also appears to have been a spirited animal requiring an extra measure of control, a martingale, which prevents the horse throwing its head back and hitting its rider in the face. The Lakenheath bridle had a two-part bit which was kinder on the horse's mouth than the Roman bit, showing humane consideration for the animal.

In both burials the horses appear to be aged between five and six, valuable animals that were far from the end of their working days. In the majority of burials it seems that age was not a consideration when a horse was sacrificed for a grave, perhaps it was considered unethical or simply bad luck to ride a dead warrior's horse, so it did not matter that the animal was buried with him. In odd cases older animals were buried like an example at Snape, Suffolk where an old horse was killed and its head buried. This animal was aged between twenty and thirty years, raising two possibilities for its placement in a grave: either it was economically sensible to bury the older animal making it a token offering or it was a much loved animal, long past its working life, but valued as a pet and therefore chosen to accompany its master to the afterlife.

In most horse burials of Saxon date they are buried with men, usually warriors of high status who were accompanied by sword, spear and shield. In the Lakenheath burial the warrior's body was in a coffin and laid beside his horse in the grave. The animal had been struck on the forehead, which may have killed it, but probably only stunned it before its throat was slit. It was then laid beside its master, still wearing its bridle and with its bucket for its feed resting nearby. In the Sutton Hoo burial the warrior was separated from his horse, though they were both contained in the same mound. The warrior's grave contained the horse's harness and its feed bucket, the horse was buried alone. In all these graves it seems the horse was important to its owner, he could not depart this life without it, in these burials we see a bond between animal and owner, rider and horse, that is familiar to all who ride today. There is a special link between a rider and his steed because when they are together they work as one, for the Saxons this was doubly important as the horse took them to battle. This bond was unbreakable, even after death.

SKULLS FOR ACOUSTICS

Ancient graves are not the only places to find horse skulls, similar discoveries have been made in houses and churches. There are numerous reports in archaeology journals of old houses being restored or repaired and floors being taken up, only for the remains of horse skulls to be found beneath. This seems to have been a common occurrence in Ireland when older cottages made from the local mud and clay were being demolished to make way for newer stone houses. The *Irish Naturalist's Journal* of 1926 records that, 'In East Limerick, most of the farmhouses up to the close of the last century were long, comparatively low, thatched structures, all built of the same type or pattern during the second half of the eighteenth century or the beginning of the nineteenth. The walls of the older houses were entirely of mud. A number of these were taken down to make way for new stone ones. In every instance where a very old house was demolished, skulls or portions of skulls of animals, horses or cows, were found, usually in the end walls.'

East Limerick was not alone. In the *Ulster Folklife* magazine of 1956 Ronald H. Buchanan wrote about visiting a house in Derrylea townland, Co. Armagh where a horse skull had been found. The skull had been situated just inside the parlour door leading from the kitchen in a rectangular hole packed with stones. It was thought the skull had been placed there before the turn of the twentieth century, but there was no real evidence to point to a date and it was possible the skull had been placed there during the building of the property in the late seventeenth and early eighteenth century. No one seemed to know why it was put there, though some believed it was to bring luck to the house.

The report sparked many more stories of similar finds. Six reports came of horse's skulls being found in barns, or rooms that were once thought to have been part of a barn. Local superstition had it that if a favoured horse died its skull should be buried beneath the barn floor and thus the barn would always be full. Perhaps we can see with this another link with the Celtic goddess Epona who was concerned with fertility, the horse personified her and it makes sense to encourage the goddess to watch over crops and keep a barn full by putting her effigy (in this case a horse skull) beneath the floor of the building. But that is supposition alone, there may have been other reasons for burying a horse's skull. Another tradition was that the skull was always buried beneath the spot in the barn where threshing was done, in several of the reports it is remarked that the skull appears to be in a spot where threshing would have been best performed. In one instance a barn had a specific threshing board in the centre of a flagged floor. When the board rotted away the horse skull was found beneath it. Again local tradition suggested this had something to do with clarifying the sound of threshing in the barn, though quite why this was important is unclear.

Horse skulls seem to be associated with good acoustics. Other Irish finds indicate there was a belief that somehow horse skulls could act as amplifiers to sound. An old man in Banbridge who died in the 1940s, had said there was a horse skull in the wall of his house supposedly put there to enable people, when sitting inside at night, to better hear anyone in the yard outside, perhaps an early security device? Though how it could possibly be effective remains a mystery. Another story recorded that in 1928 a floor was replaced in a house in Donaghcloney, Co. Down and a horse skull put under it as a piano was to stand in the room and the skull would make it sound better.

This strange custom seems to have been going on for centuries, but did it work? A Mr Craig of Gransha, Dromara helped in the rebuilding of Gransha Orange Hall in the year 1897. He had heard the stories about the acoustic properties of horse skulls and decided to experiment with the idea. He found a horse skull once belonging to a mare named Ruth and put wire through the eye sockets so he could nail the skull to the underneath of floor joists in one particular room. The results were inconclusive as some who walked on the floor 'said it did give sound and some said it did not'.

Horse skulls, it is reputed, were sometimes buried beneath choir stalls in the resonance chamber to improve the quality and sound of the singer's voices. Many churches are said to have had such skulls beneath their floor, including this one in Southwold.

Moving into England the practice seems to have been just as common and equally unfathomable. Where did the belief that skulls had acoustic properties come from? The Church seems to have been familiar with this idea as there are many tales of horse's skulls being used beneath choir stalls to enhance the sound of singing. Many older churches have resonance boxes beneath the choir, these are large hollow chambers accessed by trapdoors. The chamber's purpose was like the soundbox on a musical instrument, to strengthen and increase the volume of the singers, what benefit the horse skulls had would have been minimised by the fact that hundreds of them would have been needed to fill the deep chambers, rather than the odd few that are occasionally found.

Elsdon church in Northumberland hosts a variation on this theme. During restoration work undertaken in 1877 a box was found in the belfry, it contained three horse skulls and had been carefully secreted in a cavity in the tiny spire of the bell turret. The belfry was only erected in the seventeenth century, the skulls therefore are not relics of the medieval people who rebuilt the church around 1400. Perhaps the skulls did enhance the bell's noise as the Revd Dodgeson complained about it in the eighteenth century protesting that if the wind was blowing in the right direction the ringing could be heard for miles. Appropriately the skulls lie near the bodies of warriors, reminiscent of the Saxon graves of earlier times. The church was rebuilt after the Battle of Otterburn, when the English and the Scots clashed at the border between the two nations. The battle must have been bloody, the church was so badly damaged it seems to have been nearly entirely rebuilt and beneath its foundation rest the bodies of all those men who fell at the Battle of Otterburn. Horses and warriors reunited long after death.

Moving back into houses more evidence emerges of horses beneath floors. There were reports of a horse skull being found beneath the floor of an inn in Herefordshire, but the location now seems forgotten. Apparently the inn had flagstone floors in all rooms except one, which was the 'dancing room'. The skulls rested beneath this floor so that when people danced upon it their footsteps would resonate. Perhaps this helps explain the story of an old pub in Lowestoft, Suffolk. It is reputed that when the Three Herrings was demolished around the end of the nineteenth century, fifty or sixty horse skeletons were found beneath the floor and once more the theory is put forward that these were used as a sounding board. However, it is unlikely entire skeletons were found beneath the floor, more likely singular skulls, though it is very possible that they were numerous in number.

A more solid story also comes from Suffolk. In 1932 a local writer, Mrs Ethel Mann was staying in a house in Earsham street, Bungy, she was investigating local history and her landlady remarked to her that beneath the floor of the dining room were horses skulls. A year later Ethel had the chance to lift the floor and examine these skulls. Her discovery was remarkable, there was not just one skull beneath the floor but what she estimated to be thirty-five to forty skulls. They were arranged neatly beneath the floorboards, the teeth of each skull resting on a block of oak, some of them were so firmly wedged in place that the carpenter who was assisting her had to knock the wooden blocks aside with a hammer.

Many questions were raised by this discovery, which became quite famous in its time, it was even suggested that a Royal Veterinary College professor who hailed from Bungay might have put the skulls there, but from the start he was an unlikely suspect. Interestingly the adjoining house had also had its floors lifted and a similar discovery was made of numerous skulls. Years before these two houses had been joined, so it seemed evident that the skulls were laid down before the house was divided. A letter was printed in a local paper in March 1933 that seemed to suggest that more than one house had several skulls buried beneath its floors. The writer told the story of his grandfather who lived in a house for sixty-three years. The dining room had an asphalt floor, which was taken up and replaced with boards, beneath the boards were put around fifty horse skulls, which were thought to prevent dry rot, made the boards more resilient to the tread and clarified sounds. This happened around the middle of the nineteenth century showing how prevalent the belief still was.

Yet questions remain about the Bungay house and about the other discoveries made over the years of skulls beneath floors. Who put them there? There is no answer for that, probably the house owners either believing the skulls improved resonance or because they

Left: *In the 1930s author Ethel Mann had a floor taken up in a house in Earsham Street, Bungay, Suffolk. Beneath it were rows of horse skulls. This is her original photo of the skulls in situ. Ethel does not record what happened to the skulls after they were exposed and this photograph seems to be the only evidence that they were ever there.*

Below: *Though the custom of horse burial was discontinued after Christianity reached Britain, odd examples still survived. These usually revolved around nobility, such as Sir 'Strange' Jocelyn who was buried after his death in his grounds along with his horse. (Edwardian postcard showing a squire and his family)*

believed they brought them good luck, perhaps in an old memory of foundation sacrifices practiced in Roman and medieval times. Next is when? Surprisingly many of these skulls seemed to have been laid at a later date than the custom would suggest. The seventeenth, eighteenth and nineteenth centuries seem the commonest times, ages when pagan superstitions and practices were supposedly being eradicated. Finally the question comes, where did people get the skulls? It seems highly unlikely that these animals were intentional sacrifices, they were farmyard horses, which expired after a long and hard working life, at least that is the case with the singular skulls. When multiple bones are found beneath floors clearly they come from another source, unless a horse breeder was having a particularly bad season. Horse skulls could in fact be obtained quite easily and in large numbers from slaughterhouses where the animals were killed so that their bones could be used to make bone manure. A slaughterhouse near Kings Lynn destroyed over 50,000 horses between the years of 1800 and 1850, a grisly record, but clear proof that horse skulls could be obtained in large numbers. It could have been even easier for the owners of the Bungay house as it is thought that a slaughterhouse stood just opposite the building across the street.

Sadly for many of the animals processed by the slaughterhouses their only value was their bones. No longer the warrior's pride, no longer an effigy of Epona, their skulls were a relic of a half-forgotten tradition continued even when the people who practiced it were unclear of its meaning. Whether for acoustic purposes or good luck, by the time skulls were being buried beneath floors, the horse's skull held more importance that the living creature's body.

FIVE

THE UNICORN, MYTH AND MAGIC

THE ANCIENT UNICORN

The modern unicorn is a pure white horse with a golden horn growing from its forehead, it is usually a shy but gentle creature attracted to young maidens, it is a creature of magic and mystery, the staple of many a fantasy novel. However, if we look further back into the unicorn's past we swiftly discover a very different animal, far removed from the creatures of fairytales we are now so used to.

The unicorn's origins are hazy. Some suggest he is the product of confusion between the rhino and the oryx, developed in the mind of an ill-informed traveller. Mostly this theory rests on the fact that the rhino is the only one-horned mammal living today and that on occasion the oryx seen from the side appears to have only one horn. However, many early writers knew of both the rhino and the oryx, many scholars whilst writing of the unicorn also mentioned

In the medieval period, it was commonly thought that unicorns were a masculine symbol and therefore all unicorns were male. ('Stallion' Copyright Matthew Webber)

the rhino and oryx separately. It is more probable that the unicorn was always a symbolic creature, perhaps inheriting some of the behavioural characteristics of the rhino and oryx, but not being a derivative of these two animals.

The earliest mention of a unicorn seems to come from the Greek Ctesias, a court physician who served the Persian king, Darius II from 416 BC and later accompanied Prince Ataxerxes into battle. He returned home to Knidos seventeen years later and began composing twenty-three books on Persia and a book called *Indica*. In this last book there is a passage about the Indian unicorn, which describes it as a wild ass the size of a horse with a white body, a purple head and dark blue eyes. On its head the ass has a horn coloured white, red and black, to which Ctesias attributes many healing properties. The creature was ferocious and the only way to catch one was to wait until a herd came down to pasture with the foals, at which times hunters would surround them on horses and attempt to kill one as they could not be taken alive. The wild asses would not desert their foals and would fight tenaciously with horn and teeth, killing several hunters and horses before they were brought down with arrows. The wild ass flesh was apparently bitter and the animal was only hunted for its horn and ankle bone.

Many authors have tried to make sense of this description, analyzing it to try and dissect the animal. In truth it seems likely that Ctesias took the animal from various tales he heard, perhaps confusing the wild ass, which was hunted, with another horned animal, though the extraordinary colours of this animal call even this theory into question. Some authors suggest Ctesias may have found the multicoloured animal in Oriental silks and cloth, which were brightly coloured, again this solution is dubious.

Other travellers found their own form of unicorn; Megasthenes, a Greek official who was posted to India around 300 BC, recorded a unicorn very different to Ctesias'. His creature was the size of a horse with a mane, but dun-coloured with broad hooves, like that of the elephant's, a curly hog's tail and a sharp horn, black in colour and for the first time the horn is said to be ringed. Megasthenes unicorn was fierce, even to its own kind, very different from Ctesias' herds of unicorns. Once again, however, it seems Megasthenes was going by local tales rather than his own eyewitness account.

Many authors continued the myth, Pliny the Elder (AD 23-79) calls the unicorn the Monoceros and recounts how it is an enemy of the elephant and will spear its rival with its horn. The author Aelian, writing in AD 220, added further to the creature's description while also reiterating previous accounts. He wrote that the unicorn was a savage creature who would always attack another of its kind, fighting to the death, except during the mating season when it would behave in a docile and gentle manner towards the female. Once the mating season passed it returned to its old ferocity. Strength flowed through every part of the animal and the power of the horn was invincible. Foals were sometimes captured and taken to the king of Parsi, where they were set against each other in public shows, however, Aelian reports that no adults had ever been captured.

Once again the unicorn is seen as a powerful, ferocious creature, dangerous and hostile to others, even its own kind. The mystery of the animal's origins deepens with each new account of its behaviour. Were scholars confusing it with other animals? Alternatively, were they simply elaborating on other writers' works?

India was not the only place where unicorns could be found, though it seems to be the source for many of the later Western myths surrounding the animal. China had its own unicorn, however this was not a creature of earth but a heavenly being that would travel down to the mortal world to bestow good news. The Ch'i-Lin (also Ki-Lin) has the body of a deer, the tail of an ox and the hooves of a horse, and its forehead carries a twelve-foot-long horn with a soft tip. The Ch'i-Lin bears the sacred colours of black, white, red, blue and yellow on its back whilst its belly is brown or yellow. It is a gentle creature that causes no harm to any living thing and treads carefully through the forest lest it should step on a tiny animal. It will not even eat living grass but only that which is dead. Here we have a very different animal to the India unicorn.

The Ch'i-Lin is a solitary creature, rarely seen, though when it does appear it foretells the birth of an upright ruler. It is said the Ch'i-Lin appeared before the birth of Confucius to his mother and disgorged a jade tablet. Upon it were the words, 'son of mountain crystal, when the dynasty crumbles thou shalt rule as a throneless king'. Confucius' mother tied a ribbon round the creature's horn before it left. Seventy years later Confucius was distressed to hear that a Ch'i-Lin had been hunted and killed, the animal had still borne the piece of ribbon Confucius' mother had tied around its horn. At that point he knew his death would come soon.

Another Emperor, Genghis Khan, also encountered the Ch'i-Lin in 1224 as he was about to invade India. The creature's appearance seemed to him to be a reproach of his actions and with that in mind Genghis Khan headed home leaving India unharmed.

The Indian and Chinese unicorns are two very different creatures, one gentle and shy, the other ferocious and dangerous. They may have been creations of myth, or the product of the confusion of travellers' tales and half-remembered stories. But whatever their origins were, the authoritative stories that circulated about them greatly influenced the progression of the unicorn myth as it travelled into the Western world.

BIBLICAL BEAST

For many centuries writers, scholars and historians believed the unicorn to be a living, breathing animal, not always because of the testimony of earlier writers, who were often criticised for their elaborations, and certainly not from seeing the actual animal (though many travellers have claimed to have seen a unicorn, even in quite recent times), but because the animal was in the Bible and for many scholars that was the clinching piece of evidence. They might not agree that unicorn horn had magical properties, many even doubted the authenticity of the horns on the market, but few would claim the creature did not exist because it was recorded in the Bible and that was surely proof enough.

There is evidence in the Bible of the symbolic power of horns and specifically a single horn. In the Book of Daniel 8:1, Daniel witnesses a vision in which he sees a two horned ram with one horn longer than the other charging back and forth. No animal could stand up against him, 'He did as he pleased and became great' (Daniel 8:4). As he watched a goat approached from the west, a single horn rising from his brow and he moved across the world without ever setting foot on the ground. When he reached the two-horned ram the animals charged each other, but the one-horned goat strikes the ram with such force that both the animal's horns are shattered clean off. The ram is now powerless to defend himself and is trampled by the goat. Later when the goat is at the height of his power his horn breaks off and four more grow in its place.

The vision prophesized the coming of Alexander the Great and his destruction of the kingdom of Persia, he was the one-horned goat and when his horn broke off and was replaced by four more they stood for his successors. Here then is the symbolic nature of the horn, the ram's strength was in his horns, but the power of two horns was nothing in comparison to the strength when the pair combined into a single appendage, the focusing of the separate energies into a single horn was simply too powerful. It would seem then that the unicorn should fit into the Bible if one horn is better than two, after all God's power is awesome and invincible. 'God brought them out of Egypt; he hath as it were the strength of the unicorn' (Numbers 23:22).

Yet the unicorn has no place in the Bible despite the symbolic nature of its horn. The only reason it appears in the pages of the Old and New Testament is due to an error in translation. The mistake happened in the third century BC when seventy-two Jewish scholars were sent to the island of Pharos near Alexandria to translate the Old Testament into Greek. During the translation the learned men came across the word *re'em* in the text and struggled to find a comparative Greek word for it. They knew *re'em* referred to a mighty horned animal, but the beasts they knew seemed hardly fitting for this grand creature, the epitome of strength and power. It seems that eventually they found a substitute, the Monoceros or unicorn. This small error was perpetuated in later translations until quite recently, until the word *re'em* was reassessed and it was realised that the word probably referred to the extinct auroch or wild ox. This animal was extinct by the time of the Greek translation and unknown to the scholars, but it now replaces the unicorn in modern Bibles.

Such simple confusion of a single word resulted in the permanent establishment of the unicorn as a Christian symbol. It was partly responsible for the later medieval identification of the unicorn as Christ and led to the creation of the Holy or Mystic Hunt. One mistake turned the unicorn from a vicious wild beast into an animal of God.

THE DEVIL AND THE VIRGIN

In the Middle Ages the unicorn reached its height, through its religious connotations, through heraldry and through the supposed medicinal properties of its horn. But, initially, as the unicorn travelled into Europe it was not the revered creature it would later become, despite the Bible's endorsement. For though the Bible talks of the unicorn, for many early theologians it was unclear whether the unicorn was a good force working for the Lord or a malevolent entity in service to the Devil. Pope Gregory the Great referred to the Devil as a unicorn, but also compared the creature to Saul, who had persecuted Christians, 'but God succeeded in tethering this unicorn to the manager, fed it the fodder of the holy script, and harnessed it to his plough.' Saul became Paul.

The unicorn could still be an animal of dubious merits. Due to its inherent masculinity and the prominence of its magnificent horn the unicorn was readily associated with sexuality. Early texts that talk of the capture of a unicorn only confirm that the animal was a symbol of lust. To capture a unicorn a woman was taken out with the hunters, preferably she was a virgin, but in the earliest sources this is not necessarily a prerequisite as long as she was young and beautiful. The woman was tied naked to a tree and the hunters drew back to wait for the unicorn's appearance. When the unicorn saw the woman it would rush to her, begin licking and suckling at her breasts and become so occupied with the woman that the hunters could rush in and kill it.

Other medieval texts are even more blatant with their sexual allusions, turning the unicorn's horn into a phallic symbol and comparing it with male genitalia in not only its appearance but actions. Unsurprising then that churchmen liked to compare the unicorn to sinners, overwhelmed by earthly desires it is slain, a victim to its carnal lusts. Similarly bards in France liked to compare the unicorn to the fallen lover, a man so seduced by a woman that he cannot see the dangerous territory she lures him into.

It is hard then to fully explain how the next stage in the unicorn's symbolic development happened, for despite its sexual nature the image of the woman luring the unicorn became the basis for the Holy Hunt. In the Holy Hunt, sometimes known as the Mystic Hunt, the woman who awaits the unicorn is the Virgin Mary, and the animal himself is Christ. The logic behind this takes a moment to unravel. Usually the Holy Hunt is depicted as a single scene on altarpieces, paintings and tapestries. Mary is seen sitting within an enclosure surrounded by symbols referring to Christ's divinity. To one side, standing outside the enclosure is the angel Gabriel wearing a hunter's garb and carrying a hunter's horn. This he blows to announce the annunciation to Mary, at his feet on leads run four hunting hounds labelled as Truth, Justice, Peace and Mercy. They are driving the unicorn towards the Virgin so that he rests in her lap and Christ's spirit enters her so that the saviour might be born. Sometimes Adam and Eve appear in the same picture representing the fall from grace of mankind. Adam is sometimes seen piercing the unicorn with a spear to symbolise Christ's crucifixion, whilst a lion is usually depicted elsewhere in the scene to denote his later resurrection.

The iconography is complicated and not entirely satisfying to a modern critic. Why should Gabriel need to drive Christ in the form of a unicorn towards Mary? But in medieval art it made sense. The unicorn was a symbol of purity, the virgin a figure of chastity, the driving of the unicorn an allegory of how Christ was driven from his people and executed. It's complicated but it begins to make sense as we look at the component parts.

The unicorn was a complex beast in medieval thinking, on the one hand he was an image of Christ, his captor the Virgin Mary, on the other hand he was a symbol for sexual lust. He could even be considered an emblem of death, for in so much of the art of the time the unicorn is dying, being tormented and slain, so sometimes he can be glimpsed in scenes of the Last Judgement or chasing a person as a reminder that death stalks us all. The unicorn was all these things at once, something these days we might find difficult to comprehend, but to the medieval mind it was simple, the unicorn could be whatever you desired it to be, whatever suited your purpose best. Whether you were painting the Passion of Christ, writing a lover's sonnet, or trying to conjure an image of the mortality of life, the unicorn could be all things at once.

THE UNICORN IN HERALDRY

During the Middle Ages the art of heraldry developed. It was an age of great changes; weapons were becoming more powerful and a knight's armour had to develop too. However, with the increasing use of full helmets with visors it was becoming harder and harder for men to tell enemy and ally apart. The solution was that knights began to bear armorial patterns on their shields and on their horses.

The traditional image of the unicorn, particularly in heraldry is of a horse-like animal with a short golden beard, cloven hooves like a goat and a lion's tail. How the unicorn's appearance was created remains a mystery as does the origins of this mythical beast. (Used by permission of the Chapter of Norwich Cathedral)

This was not a new innovation, it had always been customary for opposing armies to walk under banners bearing their nations' symbols. Hengist, an early Saxon king, had a white horse on his flag and in the Bayeux Tapestry Norman knights have symbols on their shields, though it is debatable whether these signify allegiances or are just decoration. It was only later that heraldry began to mature. By the early thirteenth century heralds were employed to keep track of the shields and devices used by knights and the art of heraldry came into its own.

There was another aspect of heraldry and that was knightly behaviour or chivalry. The code of chivalry was basically a set of rules that instructed knights how to behave, for these medieval warriors, though the backbone of the army during war, could be liabilities when the country was at peace. Knights without a war grew bored, they might turn to marauding and causing trouble, worse they might start to take an interest in the politics of the king or Church. A set of rules needed to be laid down to prevent the knights from acting unethically and causing trouble. The code of chivalry was little more than a collection of guidelines for good behaviour.

Heraldic symbols were often used as allegories of chivalrous behaviour. Books were filled with these allegorical arms that used heraldic symbols to expound the knightly code. Worthy knights and troubadours in these stories carried suitable arms as they prepared for tournaments or for courting a lady.

The unicorn fitted into this ideal perfectly. The unicorn was considered a beast of great chivalry mainly because of a mythical act of purification it could supposedly perform. Many of the classical writers had recorded that animals of different species would gather

The knight adopted the unicorn as his emblem because of the creature's ferocity, pride and purity, but the animal was also featured in hunting scenes where knights chased the animal with hounds and arrows and eventually slew it. This dual nature of the unicorn, at once admired and yet also hunted, is similar to many living creatures such as the stag or wild boar.

This unicorn is from a royal coat of arms, noticeable by the crown around its neck and the chain draped about its body. Rather unusually it is grey in colour rather than the traditional white, but its mane, horn, tail and chain are all golden signifying its royal status.

by a stream to drink, but because it was believed that serpents poisoned the water, they hesitated to lap the water. Then the unicorn would walk amongst them and would dip his horn into the water, make the sign of the cross and thus purify the stream so that all the animals might drink. It was this act of kindness that was held up to be the ideal of chivalry, the mighty unicorn helping the other animals, even those it might fight with, such as the lion, to drink from the cleansed stream. This was how the knight should behave.

There were other reasons why the unicorn was such a strong heraldic emblem. Firstly, it took the form of a horse, an essential of knightly warfare on the battlefield or at a tournament. It was an animal of great strength and power, a symbol of Christ and chastity, ferocious to its enemies, a tenacious fighter, it was kind and gentle to maidens and to those in need. Its horn had magical healing properties and could thwart the poison of a serpent (an icon of the Devil). He was a proud animal, solitary and dangerous, but also a protector. There was no animal more suited to portray the knightly ideal than the unicorn.

The most famous use of the unicorn in heraldry is that in the royal coat of arms. The unicorn was introduced to the royal arms when James I came to the English throne in 1603. He brought the unicorn from the Scottish coat of arms and it seemed appropriate that the unicorn should now stand beside the lion, creatures known to be enemies, but now reconciled, just as the nations of Scotland and England were now joined. The unicorn may have a chain running between its legs, whilst the lion roars, but clearly the two old enemies are united for the greater good. Though an old nursery rhyme suggests that not all were content with the unicorn's new position:

> The lion and the unicorn
> Were fighting for the crown
> The lion chased the unicorn
> All round the town
>
> Some gave them white bread
> Some gave them brown
> Some gave them plum cake
> And drummed them out of town

THE POWER OF THE ALICORN

The unicorn's horn, or alicorn, was thought to have many medicinal properties, some considered it the only valuable portion of the animal, contesting that the rest of the body was inedible and of no use. It was because of the alicorn that the unicorn was primarily hunted, which created a problem for alicorn dealers as unicorns did not exist. There were ways round this of course, the main one being to use horns off other animals, such as the oryx, rhino and the narwhal whale. These caused critics of the unicorn to contend that either none of the horns were really from the unicorn, as they varied too widely in shape and design, or that there must be more species of the unicorn than had first been realised.

This did not stop people from buying the horn, even though it was sold at extortionate prices. This was not an issue for the buyers, as it was mainly the wealthy who felt they needed an alicorn, as it was believed the horn could detect poison and negate its effects if it had already been ingested. This remarkable property of the horn came from the many tales of the unicorn purifying poisoned waters. The horn was supposed to sweat when placed against food that was poisoned. The horn had other medicinal values, it could cure epilepsy, the plague, rabies and was good for ridding children of internal worms.

But while the existence and powers of the alicorn were not in question, many buyers were dubious about the authenticity of the horn they had just bought. James I, bringer of the Scottish unicorn, decided to test the quality of the horn he had just bought and so gave one of his servants a drink of poison containing scrapings from the horn. When the servant promptly died James contended that he had been cheated out of an authentic horn. There were other ways to test the horn, but most required someone or something to be poisoned and die. A Zurich doctor, Dr Conrad Gesner (1516-65) wrote about such a test. He stated that two doves were used and that they were both fed arsenic, then one was given a drink of unicorn horn, if this dove lived whilst the other died the horn was clearly genuine. While he was satisfied that real unicorn horn was the antidote to all poison, he was worried about the number of fakes on the market. Some of these were quite ingenious concoctions of chalk, bone and other substances, which would bubble when 'poisoned liquid' was poured onto them, thus proving they were genuine. With the growing number of fakes more tests were required; it was said that if an alicorn was used to draw a ring around a spider than the arachnid would not be able to escape it and would die within the circle. Similarly if four or five scorpions were placed in a cup with a piece of alicorn and left for some hours on returning to them they would be found all dead.

Despite the large amount of fraudulent horn, many believed they possessed the genuine article and attested to its magical healing qualities. Dr Gesner reports that he cured an epileptic by creating a draft of unicorn horn, amber, ivory scrapings, beaten gold, corals and other ingredients, which were ground coarsely and then placed in a silk sachet. He boiled down the same in water with, amongst other ingredients, cinnamon and red currants. The patient who took this draft was apparently miraculously cured. Dr Gesner also reports of a man who fearing he had eaten poisoned cherries because his stomach had distended, immediately took unicorn horn and was thus restored.

Unicorns could be seen as a symbol of chivalry, Christ and, conversely, the Devil. Yet to medieval poets they could also be a symbol of courtly love. ('Sunset Lovers' Copyright Matthew Webber)

There was of course little truth in these matters and doctors usually failed to recognise the true active ingredient in an elaborate concoction, which was beneficial to the patient, being blind-sided by such magical ingredients as the alicorn. They also failed to take into account patients recovering of their own accord, after all, who was to say the cherries were poisoned other than the man who had eaten them and who may have just been suffering from indigestion? But mistakes kept being made, another scholar experimented with kittens, feeding two of the animals with poison and then administering unicorn horn in milk to one of them. This kitten lived longer than the other, which had been given no antidote, thus the scholar concluded the alicorn had some curative properties, while failing to recognise that the milk the horn was administered in probably forestalled the poisons efficacy for a short time.

Gradually times changed. Science not only proved that all the alicorns on the market were fakes, but that the unicorn was a creature of fable. The magical, chivalrous, proud animal was reduced to a marginal figure in poetry, art and literature. Forgotten was all its great symbolism as it was turned into a mere shadow of itself, a creature remembered from half-garbled legends that did it no justice. The unicorn had lost the grandeur of its past, from its bizarre beginnings as a wild ass or heavenly Ch'i-Lin, it is transformed into a nondescript being, a horse with a horn. Some authors and artists are beginning to try to recapture the historical elegance and symbolism of this mythical marvel, but the unicorn has forever lost the medieval might of its former incarnation:

> From maiden's lap to knightly shield,
> From eastern land to western field,
> The unicorn once stood proud,
> A crown upon his head,
> Now he hides in words and paint,
> His medieval effigy growing faint,
> His crown a fading glory.

SIX

HORSE SUPERSTITIONS AND THE EVIL EYE

HORSE MAGIC

Since the earliest days of man's association with the horse, it has been believed that the animal has special powers. Some of this is down to the natural sensitivity of the horse to its environment, its heightened sense of smell and its instinctive vigilance that alerts it to potential danger sooner than a human would be. It is also a delicate animal that suffers from sudden and deadly illnesses that seem to magically appear overnight. The horse was also an animal of the gods, a symbol of the warrior, a costly animal that was an icon of wealth and status.

Until quite recently the natural world with all its marvels was a scientific mystery to most people. Animals and their habits were not entirely understood, explanations were put forward to explain

The horse was vitally important to agriculture up until the last century in Britain. The ploughman and his team would have been a familiar sight up and down the country. Farmer's feared illness in their animals, particularly when it was unexplained, they often blamed witchcraft and magic and many superstitions revolved around the well-being of the horse.

odd behaviour but were usually illogical and bizarre, at least to the modern mind. In an age when the unicorn was considered a feasible creature, it is unsurprising that its cousin, the domestic horse, should be attributed with magical powers or gifts. For example, someone sees a horse behaving fractiously, refusing to work and then if later that day a terrible storm arises the horse's strange behaviour is remembered, the animal is said to have predicted the storm. Thus superstitions are born and repeated to others until they become a fact of folklore.

Many animals were considered to have predictive powers, it is said that earlier religions of Britain used the flight patterns of birds to predict the future. Howling dogs were said to predict death, black cats passing a window indicated the arrival of a stranger, but the horse's predictive powers were not limited to just one aspect of foretelling. They could predict the weather, future prosperity, luck, the happiness of a married couple. In fact, the horse seemed able to predict almost anything:

> How superstitiously we mind our evils! The throwing down salt, or crossing of a hare, bleeding at nose, the stumbling of a horse, or singing of a cricket, are of power to daunt whole man in us.

> From the *Duchess of Malfi,* John Webster, 1623

Webster clearly knew the power of the superstition and the store people put into the predictive powers of the horse. If a horse stumbled, as Webster mentions, it was a bad portent of the future journey, especially if the rider had only just set out. It was equally a bad omen if a horse stood looking through a gateway or down a road where a prospective bride or bridegroom dwelt. The horse's stare was a sure sign that whoever resided in that direction would shortly be dead and the marriage thus filled with unhappiness. A horse neighing at the house door was a sure sign that sickness would soon infect the family. Again, these sorts of superstitions are possibly based on illogical connections between the behaviour of the animal followed by a illness or death in the family. If the opposite had occurred and good fortune had visited the family after hearing the horse neigh, the superstition would have been very different. This is seen in the black cat superstition, where some people believe the animal crossing their path is a sign of good luck, while others consider it bad luck.

Riders of piebald horses could supposedly give a cure for whooping cough if asked, according to one old superstition. Another suggests that a horse with all four feet coloured white will be no good, but Sally here, ridden by Bui is both sound and good-tempered, proving that not all superstitions can be trusted.

A superstition the horse shares with the sheep is the predictive power its offspring are alleged to have. In Suffolk it was important to take note of the first foal of the year a person saw. If the foal faced the person good luck would be with them throughout the year, however if the foal had its tail to the person the coming year did not bode well. A variant in Glasgow referred not to the foal but the plough horse. If two horses were seen working a field and their heads were turned towards the person who saw them good luck would follow, if their heads were turned away nothing but ill luck was up ahead.

The horse's magic was not entirely associated with the foretelling of people's fates. It was also considered an animal with healing powers, this was not unique to the horse, though for many other animals their healing properties were only useful after the poor creature was dead. Fortunately for the horse it was needed alive. The horse's breath was supposed to have the power to heal, a child with whooping cough would be placed underneath the horse's nose in the hope the equine would breath on it and thus restore it to health. An extension of this belief was that if a rider of a piebald horse was approached and asked for his personal cure for whooping cough he would be obliged to provide it and, if followed to the letter, the child would certainly get better. Exactly why the rider of a piebald horse should be singled out as a fountain of medical knowledge is unclear, but the piebald horse seems to be the luckiest type of horse a person could meet.

Other ailments could be cured using horse's hair. Usually the hair was employed when a person had a problem with their throat, such as a large welt or lump. Hair had to be plucked from a horse's tail, some sources specify the horse should be grey, though others do not denote any particular colour as being special. It was the procedure for obtaining the hair that was important. Another person (presumably the owner of the horse) should give nine hairs to the patient, the recipient must not say thank you nor pay for the gift. The hairs must be plaited together and then worn around the neck as a braid or placed in a bag hung round the neck and then carried until the bag wears out. How horsehair came to have this connotation is unclear, but it is not the most bizarre cure. In the sixteenth century a doctor despaired of curing his patient, Peter Lelen, who was suffering from agonising pains down his side. As a final effort to aid his patient the doctor took a large dollop of horse manure and put it in a drink of beer. From the first sip Peter seemed improved, or perhaps he was hoping the doctor would not force him to drink anymore of the vile concoction. However, Peter was 'miraculously' cured, which raises the question of just how severe the pains were in the first place.

The horse was not always the bestower of magic, unfortunately for the poor animal it could be the recipient, and usually this meant it was under the spell of a witch or evil spirit. It was said of a horse that was found sweating in its stall, wild-eyed and exhausted, that it had been hag-ridden or pixie-ridden. The animal was supposed to have been abducted in the night by a witch or a mischievous sprite, such as an elf, and ridden all night long to wherever the witch wanted to go. Thus in the morning though its stall was locked the animal was feverish and drained, unfit for work. Fortunately the witch or pixie's nightly adventures were preventable. The horse's owner had to find a hag-stone, this was usually a flint with a hole through the centre. It was hung in the horse's stall, right above the animal, so that its protective magic would cover the horse. Sometimes iron was also attached to the stone, this being a substance abhorrent to witches, they could not pass it and therefore could not get to the horses.

Hag-stones were also useful against ethereal threats, such as nightmares. The term nightmare originally referred to a form of waking dream, when a person lying in bed felt they were being suffocated by a heavy weight on their chest. *Mare* actually referred to a *maere* or *mara*, which was a form of demon that could terrorise people in their sleep. But confusion between the words and the actions of the demon apparently riding the sleeper, caused the word to become nightmare. Similarly medieval ghost stories talk of men being turned to horses and being ridden every night by demons until they are exhausted, in this case the men are actually hag-ridden. Once more the cure for this was hanging a hag-stone near a sleeper's bed so a witch or demon could not get near to transform them.

It seems the horse was embroiled in magic and witchcraft. Superstitions that faded away from other animals, seemed to linger with the horse even until quite recently. Was this due to relics of an ancient horse cult? Probably not, many of the above superstitions cannot be traced farther back than the early nineteenth century, though there are exceptions. It seems the horse has inspired an aura of magic throughout the centuries and, perhaps due to its ties with the blacksmith and his power over iron (see Chapter Seven) or simply its close dependency on mankind, and our dependency on it until relatively recently, it is a creature of healing and of good luck.

THE LUCKY HORSE

The horse was a bringer of good luck and, occasionally, bad. The luck it bestowed was not always directed at another person however; sometimes it was directly linked to the horse. It was said to be unlucky to refuse a good offer for a horse that was up for sale due to the horse's sensitivity to magic. Such an offer that was rejected would result in an accident befalling the unfortunate animal at the centre of the argument. Similarly a mare in foal should never be used to draw a funeral cart, doing so would result in the deaths of either the mare and her foal or a member of her owner's family. This type of superstition must be quite ancient, the idea that the dead should not be brought near the living, particularly the unborn or innocent child, seems to have been quite prevalent. There seems to be some belief that death can infect the living simply by them being near the corpse. Those who were young were most vulnerable to any malign influence that might come from a corpse. There is probably some element of the ghost story tied with this superstition, as it was believed, certainly in medieval times, that any person who saw a ghost would swiftly die. The horse would be especially susceptible and a valuable pregnant mare would be a significant loss to the farmer and so the superstitious kept their mares in foal away from corpses.

Other forms of ill luck could affect a foal. A horse born on Whitsuntide was terribly unlucky as it would certainly grow up to be a dangerous horse and would cause the death of someone. Horses born with four white legs were also considered to be no good, an old rhyme outlines the superstition:

> One white leg buy a horse,
> Two white legs try a horse,
> Three white legs look about a horse,
> Four white legs go without a horse.

There seems little logic behind this idea but it was a considerable worry to anyone whose mare was in foal. To prevent a horse from being born with all its legs white took some cunning. It was thought white legs were a result of a mare having the sun glaring into her eyes when she was being mated. The best way to prevent this happening was to stand the mare before a white barn wall, so her eyes were away from the sun. Assumptions could be made from this that the superstition derived from earlier myths of sun horses, but there seems no direct connection between the two myths and more than likely it was a legend that developed later in history to explain the misfortunes of genetics.

A more complicated version of the superstition was circulating in the late nineteenth century. In this instance a horse with both forelegs equally 'stockinged', that is coloured white, was deemed very lucky, however a horse with one white foreleg and one white hind leg, if both on the same side of the horse was unlucky. Completely converse to the earlier rhyme if a horse had one white leg it was unlucky, but a horse with a white foreleg and a white hind leg that was on the *opposite* side was considered lucky.

Lucky colours did not just affect prospective buyers and sellers of horses, it affected those who encountered a horse and rider on the road. As mentioned above the luckiest horse to meet was a piebald or a horse with patches of black and white on its body. To meet one piebald horse by chance brought luck, to meet two, though not together, and then to spit three times meant that the person could ask for any reasonable wish and it would be granted. More complicated versions said that the horse's tail must not be seen before the wish was carried out or that a person upon meeting a piebald horse must touch it, but only if it bore a male rider and then the person had to curtsey nine times backwards and think of a wish while she did so.

The grey or white horse could be lucky or unlucky to meet, much like the black cat. In Montgomeryshire meeting a white horse was unlucky and the only way to avert misfortune was to spit, which is a common way to avert all types of magical danger. In Herefordshire meeting a white horse would enable a person to make a wish as long as they crossed their thumbs whilst doing so. Also if the person drew a cross on their shoe a present would come their way. In Derbyshire one hundred white horses had to be spotted and counted before a wish could be made. They had to be combined with the sighting of a blind man, a fiddler and a chimney sweep (all people who are considered to have something magical either in their professions or appearance) before the wish spell was complete. This seems to have been a custom mainly followed by children and was perhaps a garbled rendition of something older.

Lastly it should be mentioned that horse riders were thought lucky, perhaps because of their connection to the horse. A bride who saw a rider on her way to church considered it a lucky omen for the future. How the horse came to possess such a plethora of luck, which it could then bestow on passers-by is a mystery. Nevertheless, in many rural counties the horse was a creature of magic and mystery. It is not mentioned how often a horse was met and no luck followed to cheer the onlooker, but very often we create our own luck. If we see something that bodes good fortune we will be more receptive to anything 'lucky' that comes our way and will attribute any sudden opportunity or exciting news to the lucky omen we had previously seen. A similar thing can be seen to happen with bad luck, people are waiting for it to happen. Maybe this creates some superstitions, but it is still a mystery why our ancestors held such stock in the luck brought about by the horse.

HORSESHOES AND HORSEBRASSES

The horseshoe could be said to be one of the ultimate icons of luck. Who does not know that a horseshoe is lucky? It appears on cards and cakes to celebrate birthdays, christenings and marriages; it is thrown as confetti, horseshoe-shaped pendants hang round people's necks, or appear on brooches, all to ensure the person does fall foul of misfortune. Why is the horseshoe such an icon? Truly, no one has yet answered that question though it no doubt draws some of its magical quality from its manufacture. It is made of iron, a material repugnant to evil spirits and is forged by a blacksmith who himself was said to possess magical qualities. It is unknown how long the horseshoe has been considered a lucky item; however, an early mention comes from a fourteenth-century manuscript. Initially it was good luck just to find a horseshoe, and it did have to be a *found* shoe, one that was bought new had not acquired the magic of luck, which presumably was translated to it through the horse. Preferably, the horseshoe would still have a nail in it from when it was attached to the horse's hoof, these nails could be significant, they would indicate the number of years the horseshoe would bestow luck on its finder. No nails meant there was no luck left. Equally the gaps where nails were missing would tell the person how many years they had before they would be married, though what they indicated if a person was already wed is not mentioned.

The most common use for the horseshoe was to protect a person against witchcraft. If a girl was lucky enough to find three horseshoes in one year and threw them over her left shoulder she would never be enchanted by witchcraft. Also if a shoe was found, spat on and thrown over the shoulder it was good fortune. This most likely stems from the belief that the Devil looks over a person's left shoulder and by throwing the iron horseshoe behind them the person is hoping to strike the Devil, iron being as adverse to the Devil as to witches.

The horseshoe is a universal icon of luck, but much debate goes on about which way up it should be hung. These shoes are all hung with points down to pin down the luck or the Devil, so he can't cause mischief. Others would aver that hanging shoes in such a manner only allows all the luck to run out!

Horseshoes were being nailed at thresholds to exclude demons and witches as early as the sixteenth century. If a woman was suspected of being a witch a horseshoe might be nailed to her door to test her, if she could not leave because of the iron she was clearly a witch. The practice was quite common and not just in rural communities but in London and other city centres. The horseshoe was also a cure-all for the supposed ills of witchcraft. A person might carry the nails from the single shoe of a stallion to keep him safe from magic. While any person who discovered that their milk would not become butter would believe it had been bewitched, and the only cure for this was to heat a horseshoe and dip it in the milk to break the charm.

Arguments arise when the positioning of a horseshoe is debated. Some authorities insist the shoe must be points down, to pin in the luck or to trap the devil. It is also suggested that this is the ideal position because when a witch or devil attempt to enter the house they fly into the horseshoe, are swept round in a circle, and turned back to the way they came. Thus they could never enter.

On the other hand some argue a horseshoe must be placed points up to prevent the luck from running out or to catch the luck. However, there seems to be no hard or fast rule and many early sources did not specify the position a horseshoe should be nailed in, so presumably it was not important. Nowadays on cards, cakes and jewellery the horseshoe can appear both ways up depending on the artistic bent of the designer. The symbol of the horseshoe is what is now deemed important.

Whilst the horseshoe was used to protect people from witchcraft, the horse brass was used to protect the horse. The original function of the horse brass was as a protection against the Evil Eye, a form of magic. Some people were said to have the Evil Eye, they were perhaps old ladies who lived alone and therefore prime suspects in witchcraft, someone who rolled up their eyes, or stared hard at a person could be said to be inflicting the Evil Eye. Anyone with different coloured eyes was presumed to have such an ability. A person was not always aware they had the power whilst others would encourage those to believe they could curse them with a look, to inspire fear.

Horses were deemed particularly prone to being affected by the Evil Eye, they could be easily 'overlooked' or have spells cast upon them, this was why it was considered unlucky to refuse a good offer for a horse, as the prospective buyer might inflict the Evil Eye on the horse. Envy is usually the cause of such magic; the Evil Eye was laid upon those who seemed to be doing well or at least better than the jealous onlooker was. This was why the power was most feared at rural shows when the animals might be in triumph or looking grand, thus arousing more jealousy in a person. A way to divert the Evil Eye was necessary and since it was the first glance of the malicious person

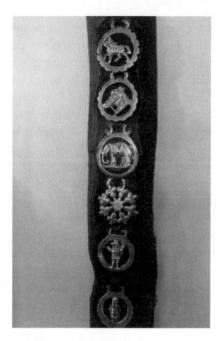

Horse brasses were designed to attract the Evil Eye and deflect it from its intended victim, but later they became a collector's item such as these that hang in the Huntsman and Hounds pub in Wissett, Suffolk. There are many designs including animals, mythological figures, buildings and royalty, those that are old and have actually been worn by a horse are particularly popular.

that was most deadly it needed to be attracted away quickly. The eye was drawn to shiny objects that caught the light, horse brasses when highly polished and hung all over the equine would distract the Evil Eye and its influence would be diverted.

How ancient the superstition of the horse brass is, seems impossible to tell. It may have arisen when the first horses brasses were being worn in the Iron Age, finds of which have been made in The Park of the Horses, Abergele, or they may have not held any particular meaning until the medieval period or even later.

Perhaps, like so many other superstitions, they are a product of the eighteenth and nineteenth centuries. However, supposition with no supporting evidence leads us only round in circles. What is clear about the horse brass is that in the nineteenth century, with mass production, it reached its height. Thousands of different designs have been made over the years, from agricultural scenes, to symbolic motifs. Some of these designs are said to have their own special significance:

The Anchor. Symbol of St Nicholas, patron saint of sailors and children.

Arrow Heads. This were based on finds of flint arrow heads that were thought to be of fairy origin and were known as 'elf bolts'. Original flint arrow heads were mounted and worn as charms.

The Bishop's Mitre. The shape of the mitre protected against evil influence and frightened people with evil intent.

The Cockerel. A symbol of vigilance and also with the interest in the game of cockfighting, a symbol of tenacity in battle.

The Cross. A rare design due to the Catholic Church's disapproval of amulets. Usually the cross is depicted as the Maltese cross and is another symbol of protection.

The Dog. A symbol of loyalty and friendship, and also the popular pursuit of hunting.

The Fox. A lucky charm explained by an old rhyme, '*I ham a cunen Fox you see; Ther is no harm attached to me; It is my Masters wisch to place me here; To let you know he doth not fear.*'

Horse's Hoof. A symbol of good luck and another measure to prevent the animal being hag-ridden.

The greatest danger of becoming the victim of the Evil Eye was during a fête or show, when the target was in triumph as the eye was a result of jealousy. At such events as this fête it was important that the horse was grandly turned out with many shiny objects adorning its harness, so the eye would not be able to rest on its intended victim. (Edwardian postcard of horse and float)

This is far from being a comprehensive list of designs and there are many more not just made and used for symbolic purposes, but for ornamentation. The beauty of a horse fully harnessed with horse brasses hanging on the straps is becoming a rarer sight today, apart from at agricultural shows. It is hard to imagine that horses brasses were ever solely used for defence against the Evil Eye, they are simply too decorative and must have been as equally cherished for ornamentation. These days it is more common to see a horse brass hanging on a pub fireplace than on a horse, but perhaps there, as they sparkle in the sunlight of a summer's afternoon, they might still distract that malicious wandering eye and allow us to drink our slowly warming pints in peace.

CRYING THE MARE

The last custom to be mentioned in this chapter is that of Crying the Mare, possibly a fertility custom associated with corn spirits. How widespread the custom was or is remains debatable. It was definitely practiced in Hertfordshire and Shropshire and no doubt in other areas of the country. Crying the Mare was associated with harvesting. It was a competition to see who would be first to reap all their corn and no one desired to be last. When the corn was nearly completely reaped a ceremony was performed. The last stand of corn was tied into four bunches representing the legs of the horse and then the tops of the corn were pulled together and tied. This was the mare and the reapers would all gather to one side and attempt to cut one of the legs of the horse by throwing their scythes at the corn. The successful reaper was honoured at the evening's harvest feast by being allowed to sit next to his master.

When the horse was cut cries went up declaring where the corn horse would now flee to since her field had been reaped. The name of a farmer who was behind in his harvest would be shouted out. The mare was often said to be 'sent' to this lax farmer to help him with the harvest, sometimes the man might play up to the joke and appear at the reaped field with a bridle, at other times a real horse was sent to the farm behind in its harvest, bedecked with ribbons. The man who was last to harvest his fields was said to retain the mare over the winter, though there seems little indication of what result this might have on his farm.

Several older sources claim this is a corn spirit rite. The spirit was thought to reside in the field during the summer and when the corn came to be cut the spirit was effectively kicked out of its home. The mentioning of the farmer whose fields remained untouched by the scythes is perhaps to tell the spirit where it is to flee to; naturally, it would head to the next nearest cornfield. However, much of this custom seems to be less about a supernatural entity and more about jovial competition in a farming community. Could the corn mare not represent the real horses used to help carry away the corn? The crying is perhaps a symbolic gesture of triumph, of mockery also, the handing over the mare to the next farmer is a joke against his slowness to complete the harvest.

Perhaps, like the horse brasses, we are trying to see too much meaning in a custom that was primarily about competition. There is no doubt that the horse is a creature once deemed magical, but to see every tradition as an extension of this magic is perhaps taking the idea too far.

The horse played a large role in the world of agriculture, war, sport and transport, until very recently. It was not as expendable as the dog, because of the cost to rear and train a decent horse. It was not an icon of witchcraft like the cat, instead it was a creature harassed by perceived magic, prone to unaccountable illnesses and quirks in behaviour. Still today the horse engenders feelings of companionship, trust and loyalty, such qualities our forebears also cherished. Perhaps we should not be surprised that in past centuries the horse, so closely linked with humans, should become a focus for superstitions. Wars were won on the backs of horses, literally. Perhaps that is why they were considered so lucky, their role in our lives has encompassed so many things and there is still something mysterious about the horse, something undefined. Perhaps even something magical.

CHAPTER SEVEN

MAGIC IN THE BLACKSMITHS

MAGIC METAL

Iron came to Britain around the fifth century BC; before then the metal of choice was bronze, an expensive and soft material, used mainly by the wealthier members of society for weapons and tools. Initially iron did not replace bronze, it took some time for the metal workers to understand the correct process of smelting and forging the new material to create a superior weapon. It was with this new development, and the replacement of cast weapons with forged weapons, that the role of the blacksmith arose.

The first craftsmen who experimented with this novel material had much to learn. Iron is highly malleable when heated, it can be forged and re-heated almost indefinitely, until the metal forms the precise shape required. No doubt, the ordinary man or woman watching the blacksmith at his work would have marvelled at his control over this new material, how he shaped it to his will. The blacksmiths themselves soon took to keeping their techniques secret, sharing them only with those learning the craft, so the smith took on an aura of a mystic, a man who worked metal with formidable skill.

Iron was, and is, such a versatile material. It could be shaped into weapons, tools, ornaments, pans and decorative objects; in reality there was little it could not be used for. This phenomenal metal, which could replace many of the tools commonly made of wood, gave the blacksmiths an unrivalled place amongst their fellows. They were indispensable. Without them other tasks could not be completed, the knife for cooking, the sword for battle, the plough shears for farming; even in much later times the smith was considered the hub of a community and without him many could not complete their work.

However, there were those who were less than enthralled with this new material. Hesiod the Greek considered it evil. Herodotus believed it brought harm to humankind. Ovid argued that the earth hid iron beneath the soil because it was a material of evil, and only misfortune and destruction could come from its removal and forging. Some of these arguments were not entirely illogical, after all iron had enabled the development of better weapons for war, the sword, axe and spear were now hardened in the dark metal, more dangerous than ever. Many would consider the unearthing of such a material, so ideally suited to war, an act of destruction and evil.

Over the centuries iron has played as large a part in agricultural and peaceful life as it has in bloodshed and battle. It was commonly believed that it could protect against evil. Horseshoes were the most common charm against ill luck and mischief, (see Chapter Six) but any object made of the metal was thought to possess special qualities. To protect a newborn child from being snatched away by elves a piece of iron and the father's coat would be placed at the foot of the bed where mother and child slept. If the child slept in a crib, similar protection could be achieved if a knife or pair of scissors was laid nearby.

Other iron superstitions included the drawing of three circles in the air around a person and then three on the ground enclosing the feet using an iron weapon. This was a strong protection against the evils of witchcraft. Irons nails driven into a house kept out plague. Interestingly, iron buried beneath an ash tree would have its magic drawn into the living tree and the following year any cattle affected by the influence of the Evil Eye would be cured if they would stood beneath the tree. Why iron was considered such a protective material is uncertain. Certainly, from its very beginning its working and the craftsmen who have shaped it, have been considered gifted with magic. The smith was to all intents and purposes a magician, conjuring blades and decorations from raw metal, using another power that was considered to have magical qualities, fire. In fact fire is also considered able to purify atmospheres of evil, unfortunately, this was why some people were burnt at the stake, to purify their souls. So perhaps it is the combination of fire and iron that has created the abundance of superstitions surrounding the metal. Or perhaps fairies really are allergic to iron.

SMITH GODS

Superstition surrounded the blacksmith from early in his career, so it is perhaps unsurprising that smiths were as important in mythology as they were in real life. Mythical smiths included the Roman

Vulcan who used a volcano as his forge and fashioned weapons and lightning bolts. Vulcan's Greek equivalent was Hephaestos, the lame son of Zeus. His father, so ashamed and angered at his deformed son, cast him from Olympus where he landed in the sea. Despite his withered legs he was a talented craftsmen and excelled at metalwork, he later used his smith skills to trick his way back into Olympus and eventually married the goddess Aphrodite.

Closer to home the Celts had their own collection of smith gods. In Wales there was the smith god Govannon, one of the many children of the goddess Don, like most mythical smiths he had prowess over forged weapons and was once made to craft weapons for one of King Arthur's knights, Culhwch, who had been challenged to commission the weapons from the smith god by the giant Yspaddaden. Govannon had a darker side though, and murdered his newborn nephew, the sea deity Dylan. All the waves wept at the smith's callous act.

Govannon's Irish counterpart was Goibniu, who was famous for his role in the Second Battle of Moytura. The Danaans were warring against the Fomorians, a battle they probably would not have won had they not had Goibniu on their side. During the battle the smith speedily fashioned swords and spears, each requiring only three blows from his hammer. He was assisted by Luchta the carpenter who crafted the handles and only needed to throw them at the spear heads to have them fasten together. Also assisting was Credne the goldsmith who would toss rivets at the spears as fast as he struck them, and they would fasten immediately in place. It is said the night before the battle a Fomori spy crept up on Goibniu to steal the secrets of smith craft and injured the god. But this seems not to have hampered the smith when he forged the Danaans' weapons.

Yet another Irish smith deity was Culann, who was considered a reincarnation of the sea god Manannan Mac Lir. He possessed a massive hound that guarded him. The young Setanta killed it when the guard dog attacked him. Needless to say Culann was furious about the slaying of his dog and to make restitution Setanta offered to replace the hound with himself. Culann agreed and Setanta's name was changed to Cuchulann 'The Hound of Culann'.

When the Anglo Saxons arrived they too brought a smith god, this was Wayland (sometimes known as Volund). He was also known in Scandinavian tradition. His mother was a mermaid, his father the sea giant Wate and he was an accomplished smith working with dwarfs as an apprentice to the blacksmith Mimir. His skills soon surpassed the dwarfs and rumours began to spread about his talents. He lived for seven years in Ulfdaler, but was then captured by the Swedish king Nidude, who wanted him to work in his royal forge. To prevent Wayland escaping the king had him hamstrung.

The result of his capture and torment was a burning desire for revenge within the smith, which smouldered inside him as he worked at the royal forge. He bided his time and then one day when king Nidude's two sons came to view the treasures Wayland had made, he murdered them. He turned their skulls into drinking cups encrusted with precious jewels and mounted on silver, which he then sent to Nidude. It seems that this terrible act did not deter the king from keeping his smith, nor did it stop his daughter, Bodvild, from visiting Wayland to have a ring repaired. Once she was in his forge Wayland raped the girl and then escaped on wings he had fashioned from birds' feathers and, in Scandinavian versions, ended up in Valhalla.

Wayland's smithy is situated in Wiltshire near the Uffington horse. It is a long barrow reputed to be his burial chamber and it is mentioned as early as AD 850. Local legend has it that any horse will be shoed by the smith's spirit if a coin is left on a stone near the barrow. The horse must be left on its own near the site and as long as the rider does not attempt to watch the smith at work, his horse will be shoed in the morning.

Finally there is the Celtic legend of the Island of the Big Blacksmiths. The Celtic adventurer Maildun discovered this isle whilst sailing the oceans. He and his crew first approached the island and heard giant bellows pumping and the loud strikes of hammers dealing blows to a glowing lump of iron on an anvil. The island was inhabited by giant blacksmiths who seemed to intend to capture Maildun and his men. He realised this, fortunately, before he landed and ordered his men to start rowing their boat backwards to escape the giants. The blacksmiths guessed their plan and one rushed out of the forge with a lump of red-hot iron grasped in his tongs. He flung the iron at the hero and his crew, but thankfully it fell short, sinking into the hissing and boiling waves as Maildun hastily made his retreat.

CHRISTIAN IRON

It was not just pagan deities who were associated with the craft of the blacksmith, with the coming of Christianity, saints began to be associated with the art of forging metal. The patron saint of blacksmiths is St Eloi (also Eloy, Loy or Eligius), who was born at Chaptelat, near

Limoges in AD 588. He served as an apprentice to a goldsmith, before moving to Paris and working as a treasurer to king Clotaire II. It was for his patron that he built two magnificent thrones. When Clotaire died Eloi was allowed to retire from royal society and founded a monastery in Limousin, later he also established a nunnery in Paris.

He became famous as a craftsman creating various treasures in metal for his king. It was probably this renown that led to the legend that has linked him eternally with the art of the blacksmith. The tale states that Eloi was working in his forge one day when a horse was brought to him to be shoed. The animal was intractable and believed to be possessed of the Devil, it refused to stand patiently whilst Eloi tried to shoe it, and it soon became clear it could not be shod in the usual manner. Eloi however, without hesitation cut off the leg that needed to be shoed, took it to his anvil and forge, shaped the shoe, nailed it to the hoof and then returned the leg to the horse, neatly stitching the severed limb back to the animal by making the sign of the cross. An addition to the legend furthers the miraculous feat, saying that Eloi removed all the horse's legs and shod them before reattaching them to the animal. A man was passing and saw this strange operation, determined to mimic the saint's triumphs he cut off the horse's legs, resulting in the animal's death. Eloi crossly accosted the man, and used his saintly powers to restore the horse to life.

Many paintings and sculptures of St Eloi portray him holding a horse's severed limb, or shoeing it at his forge. Sometimes a horse stands nearby patiently waiting for its leg to be returned. He was very popular, particularly in France during the Middle Ages, when his feast was celebrated on the first day of December. He was clearly quite popular in Britain also as his portrait appears in churches in

Wiltshire, Somerset, Dorset and Suffolk. He also gets a mention in Chaucer's *Canterbury Tales* during the prologue when the Nun enjoys using the oath 'By Saint Loy!'

A smith saint of British origin is St Dunstan. Famously he shod the Devil. Dunstan was born in AD 910 near Glastonbury. He was from a noble family and was sent to the court of King Athelstan, but trouble soon brewed as Dunstan was accused of dabbling in black magic and was expelled from court. It is thought that many of the tales about Dunstan's battles with the Devil are in fact allegories of his own conversion to Christianity through his uncle St Alphege. Whether Dunstan did toy with the dark arts of the Occult is unknown, but he was converted and became a Christian. He travelled back to Glastonbury and built himself a small cell next to the church where he could pray and make sacred vessels and bells for the church. To facilitate his craft he had a forge installed in his cell and spent long hours working beside it.

One night Dunstan was working at his forge when a beautiful young woman walked into his small cell. She attempted to seduce him, dancing round his forge, but Dunstan refused to look up from his work. The woman grew impatient and as she danced round the room her skirts flew up revealing the cloven feet of the Devil. Dunstan now knowing for certain who had been tormenting him, swung round with a pair of red-hot tongs and clamped them round the woman's nose. The Devil's terrible howls roused the whole neighbourhood and broke the stone upon which Dunstan's cell rested into three pieces. The demon disappeared into the night. In some versions, the scene of this incident is Mayfield, Sussex and when the Devil flees, racing across the sky, he sees the springs of

Tunbridge Wells and, desperate to soothe his burning nose, plunges it into the stream. This is the reason given for the red colouration of the water and its taste of sulphur.

A slightly different account relates that the Devil did not come to St Dunstan to seduce him but to ask the clergyman to shoe the fallen angel's cloven feet. Not fooled by the Devil the saint ties him to a wall and shoes him, causing the creature great pain. The Devil begs to be released, but Dunstan will only ascent if the Devil promises never to enter a house with a horseshoe displayed outside. Apparently, the Devil agrees and is released. This is probably another legend that has been created to give an explanation to the widespread superstition that horseshoes warded off the Devil.

Other saints are associated with horses and smiths for other reasons. St Patrick helped a smith overcome a swindling publican, though the smith was under the mistaken impression that Patrick was a Druid high priest. St Clement was a bystander when a blacksmith found King Alfred in his forge causing havoc, after the smith had gone 'on strike' for being passed over when the king was naming the greatest craftsmen in his kingdom. On St Stephen's day, horses were bled to ensure their health for the following year. St Martin was considered the patron saint of any traveller riding on horseback and in the Middle Ages when a rider was going on a long journey he would have an extra shoe made for his horse. This was hung at home to ensure Martin's protection. St Clement is also sometimes considered the patron saint of blacksmiths because his symbol is an anvil. On St Clement's day, 23 November, smiths celebrated by exploding gunpowder on their anvils and having a parade with an effigy of St Clement as the chief figure. On the other hand

St Egwin is someone smiths might like to avoid as once, when he was attempting to preach to the smiths of Warwickshire and they were ignoring them and striking their hammers on their anvils, he prayed to God that they would be destroyed – and they were.

CURSES AND CURES

A good blacksmith must not only be able to work metal but to be able to control large and unruly horses. In days gone by he would also have certain veterinary talents, he would know how to make special shoes that would help a horse with leg ailments, sometimes having to be highly inventive to cure a defect in the horse's hoof. He could make a clever shoe that would stop a horse with Knock-knees from bending its legs, by adjusting the depth and width of the shoe. This was a handy trick when the horse was about to be shown, similarly special shoes would be made to make a working horse's feet look bigger for competition.

The skill a smith showed over horses meant he fell into the same category as certain kinds of horsemen and gipsies. He would have 'trade secrets' that enabled him to tame wily horses and people would suspiciously wonder just what those secrets were. In centuries past people would have quickly made the leap to magic, some horsemen actively encouraged this idea as it made them renowned, respected and no doubt feared. In 1664 Thomas Lindsay was accused of witchcraft having boasted that he could stop a horse in the midst of pulling a plough by turning widdershins (contrary to the course of the sun) and giving a word of command. But the horsemen and smiths' 'gifts'

The blacksmith's shop and forge was the traditional centre of a village or town – at one time or another everyone would have to stop by the smithy, whether to mend an old iron pot or a gardening implement. A blacksmith was said to be a highly reliable guide to the temperament and quality of a horse, working with them so closely as he did, he was also able to correct faults in a horse's legs or carriage by making special shoes.

were in actuality down to a good understanding of the horse and its temperament. Some of these horsemen would be thought of as horse whisperers today, they understood the horse's body language and knew how to calm an animal, some were highly adept at this skill.

Other methods of horse control involved pungent lotions that could be surreptitiously dabbed onto a horse's nose. The smell was so obnoxious to the horse that it would stand stock still, no matter how its owner tried to persuade it to move, until the scent was neutralised using a different concoction, a usual one being milk. The smith no doubt knew of such substances, there were various recipes circulating of the best mixture, though most still involved a heavy dose of magic thrown in for good measure, such as the collecting of ingredients at night and the saying of special words.

Such magic, whether for show or truly believed by the performer, caused the blacksmith to be feared and respected by his fellows. It was not just because they believed that the smith could curse or cure a person by turning his anvil in different directions, but because the forge and its workers were the hub of a village. Without the smith many other industries could not go on, and this is demonstrated in a legend that was related yearly at the Feast of St Clement. The story is known as the King and the Blacksmith, sometimes the king is Solomon, though more usually Alfred. The legend goes that Alfred gathered together the finest craftsmen in his kingdom to decide of all the trades which should be know as the greatest. Representatives of each trade came to the king and presented their finest goods. Alfred was having a difficult time deciding who should be classed the 'prince of all craftsmen', but when he saw the fabulous coat a tailor had made he instantly decided that he would get the title.

The Normans seem to have been the first to insist all horses should be shod, good practice, until a horse throws a shoe and also a rider, as is said to have happened to William the Conqueror with the result that he eventually died from his injuries. (Used by Permission of the Chapter of Norwich Cathedral)

The smithy would have been a smoky place from the huge forge fires, the steam from dipping hot metal in cooling water and from the placing of hot shoes onto the horse's feet. The smoke produced during this smells like burning hair, a rather pungent and lasting smell.

The blacksmith (who in some versions is further dishonoured by not being invited by the king to attend) was angered by this choice, which had obviously been swayed by the gaudy appearance of the coat rather than the skill of the worker. He declared that he would do no work until he was crowned 'prince of all craftsmen'. At first this threat seemed minor, but time passed, the metal tools of the other craftsmen needed repairing and then the king's horse lost a shoe. However, the smith would not relent and go back to work. In desperate need of tools, the craftsmen and king Alfred broke into the forge and tried to repair their own tools. In the chaos that followed an anvil was knocked over and exploded. The smith hearing the commotion rushed to his forge, at his side came St Clement and when they entered the smithy they were both appalled at the mess the other craftsmen had created. The king, knowing he had no choice but to rescind his previous judgement, agrees that the smith is the true 'prince of all craftsmen' and begs him to return to work. The blacksmith was overjoyed and immediately began work again.

The tailor however, peeved at this development and that night was at a feast held in the smith's honour, he snuck under the table and snipped tiny cuts into the bottom of the smith's apron. It said that up until the last century smiths still wore fringed aprons in remembrance of this act of spite from the tailor.

At least the king's story had a happy ending, such was not the case in the story of the curse of Nether Lypiatt Manor in the Cotswolds, once the home of Prince and Princess Michael of Kent. The curse dates back to the seventeenth century when Judge Coxe built the property. He was a notorious man and it was because of his actions

In days gone by the smith did not just shoe horses. The sign above this smithy states, 'J. E. Skinner Smith and Coach Builder, Agent for Agricultural Implements'. All these trades are now gone but the role of the smith as a farrier still exists. Notice also the horseshoe-shaped doorway of the smithy, many of the older buildings incorporated such a design. (Early twentieth-century postcard, 'The Smithy, Penshurst, Kent')

The modern blacksmith is usually mobile, going from horse to horse, rather than having his customers come to him. But the tools of his trade have not changed, he still has an anvil and hammer and file. Comparing the last two pictures it can be seen that very little of the art of shoeing horses has changed at all over the centuries.

that his home was cursed. The story begins when Judge Coxe hired a local blacksmith to make the fine iron gates that still stand in front of the house. Work on the gates was abruptly halted when the blacksmith was arrested and convicted of stealing sheep, a crime that in those days carried a death penalty. The presiding judge was none other than Coxe and he saw no reason why, just because the man was going to be hanged, his gates should be left unfinished. Therefore, he postponed the execution until the smith finished his work. An awful task it must have been for the smith knowing that as he forged each piece of metal he was drawing closer and closer to his own death, no wonder than that he thought of revenge. It is said he worked a deliberate mistake into the design of the gates, one that can only be noticed upon close examination, and, more dramatically, he is said to have cursed Judge Coxe and his new home.

Many Cotswold people believe that the curse still lingers round Nether Lypiatt preventing the house from ever passing from father to son. This pattern began almost immediately as Judge Coxe's own son hanged himself in one of the rooms and subsequently no son has inherited the property. Even in recent years, the house seems to have had a large turnover of owners despite its picturesque setting in the attractive Cotswolds area. A strange story of a blacksmith who had his forge invaded by a ghost metal worker comes from Cradley Heath in Worcestershire. The forge resided in a place called Lomey Town and early one morning in 1868 the smith went down to his workshop and found the ashes from the previous day's fire scattered across the floor. Passing it off as the work of local pranksters, he stayed up the next night to catch them in the act. He was awoken during his vigil not to see youths who had snuck into his forge, but a ghostly figure that was raking the red-hot ashes from the fire and scattering them onto the floor using its bare hands. Having finished the bizarre task it walked through a wall and disappeared. The smithy was subsequently considered haunted and no local residents would walk past it at night, though what explanation there could be for the mysterious appearance was never discovered.

More bizarre is a tale that firmly fixes the blacksmith's place in the annals of magic and myth. The legend comes from Lochaber,

Inverness, and relates how a smith came upon and captured a *Glaistig*, an evil fairy creature that was half-woman, half-goat. He would only release her if she gave him a herd of cattle. Immediately the cattle were produced and the smith made another demand, he desired a house that no fairy or enemy could enter. Once more the *Glaistig* complied and summoned goblins to come forth and build the property, a task they completed within one night. Finally the smith released her and she stuck out her hand in farewell, but rather than allow the evil creature to roam freely again the smith took a red-hot iron from his fire and seared her hand. In agony the *Glaistig* fled to the Hill of Finisgeig where she bled to death. It is said the vegetation on the hill is still red in the spot where she died.

From all these tales it is clear that the blacksmith was a man of marvels and magic. He could bring a curse down upon a family, or help a horse win a competition with carefully crafted shoes. He knew the tricks to calm a horse and how to work iron with skill and finesse. He was the hub of a village, the place where all metal tools at one time must pass through. His role with the horse entwines him with ancient mythology, with the secrets of horsemanship that are centuries old. Before there were horse whisperers and animal behaviourists, there was the blacksmith, who knew his way around a horse better than some owners did. Though these days it is rare to see a forge, most smiths being mobile with vans that serve as roadworthy smithies, the heritage of the old iron workers is not forgotten, nor will it ever be, as long as a horse needs shoes and there is a man who can forge them.

EIGHT

HIGHWAYMEN AND
SPECTRAL HORSES

THE HIGHWAY HORSE

For the highwayman a horse was indispensable, it was what made him stand above the footpad and ordinary thief, it was what made him a 'gentleman of the road.' Legends circulated about magical horses that could carry a highwayman far away from the scene of his crime, could help him elude any guards or soldiers set to chase him; the myths surrounding the power of these horses were akin to the old Celtic stories of horses that wept or that could carry ten men at the same time. However, despite the accolade and reputation the public gave these horses, very often they were treated with disregard or even cruelty at the hands of their owners. Many were stolen, a highwayman changing horses as frequently as he could for there was a great danger that a 'borrowed' horse might be recognised by its real owner and the highwayman captured. Some highwaymen tried to disguise their animals, giving them false tails or covering their heads with cat furs to make them appear a different colour. Yet it seems the biggest weakness in the highwayman's schemes was often his horse.

Many recognised not only the potential for a horse to reveal its master's true occupation, but also the ability the animal gave to others for pursuit and capture of the highwayman. When 'Captain' James Hind held up a carriage in the seventeenth century he shot all six of its horses to prevent anyone following him. It is this same Hind who was reputed to feed flesh to his own horse to improve its stamina and strength. Others adopted similarly barbaric practices to prevent themselves being followed. When a gang robbed a stage-coach transporting £15,000 from Manchester to London in 1692 they stabbed sixteen of its horses and drove away the remainder. Other highwayman took the simpler, and far less cruel, precaution of cutting the girths and bridles of their victims' horses.

Even the most famous act of kinship between a horse and highwayman, that between Dick Turpin and Black Bess, is completely fictional. The bond between the pair was created by Harrison Ainsworth in his book Rookwood – he invented Black Bess and her almost supernatural ability to carry Dick miles away from a crime scene and render him with an alibi as people thought it impossible that he could have ridden such a distance so swiftly. Black Bess was intelligent, brave-hearted and intuitive, so in tune with her master that she sacrificed her life to afford him an alibi, making a desperate ride to York where she dies on the road in sight of the city. Turpin weeps for his lost friend, a tragic end for the graceful steed. In reality

Turpin was a cruel thug unlikely to have wept for his horse. He stole his steeds regularly getting rid of them as soon as they became recognised. Black Bess is little more than a writer's invention to give an otherwise heinous and villainous character a touch of empathy and humanity. Even the ride to York, so widely attributed to Turpin, was made by a different highwayman entirely, William Nevison, who became known as Swift Nick because of his exploit. He made the journey to give himself an alibi for a robbery in Kent, travelling approximately 200 miles. It is uncertain whether he used only a single horse or he changed them regularly, but the result was that he obtained an alibi. Unfortunately, for him, his legendary exploit was later hi-jacked by Turpin.

Despite this list of animal cruelties there seem to have been some highwaymen that, at least in their legends, appear to have had a kinship with their horses. Among them is another highwayman whose life was fictionalised by a later author. R.B. Blackmoore included the real-life Tom Faggus in his book Lorna Doone, using local folklore to bulk out the character and provide him with his magical horse 'Winny'. Faggus' horse was so well trained that people came to believe that Faggus was a wizard and his horse, his familiar. Some went even as far to say that if his horse had not been shot first Faggus would never have been caught.

A horse of similar repute belonged to 'Wild' Humphrey Kynaston (1474-1534) in Shropshire and haunted the road between Shrewsbury and Oswestry. He was a true 'gentleman' thief having been born a member of the landed gentry and inheriting Myddle Castle when his father died in 1517. He began his life on the road when he was outlawed by Henry VII for committing murder. Legend has it that

Player's Navy Cut Cigarettes.

THE HIGHWAYMAN

The highwayman was a romanticised criminal, 'the gentleman of the road'. He was often bloodthirsty and ruthless, but in popular fiction of the time he was transformed into a lovable rogue, and was often accompanied by an equally fictitious steed, such as Black Bess. In actuality, most highwaymen stole their horses and changed them regular for fear of detection.

he moved into a cave in Nesscliffe rock, a place that can still be visited today. To reach his hideaway Kynaston climbed a set of steep steps cut into the stone followed by his faithful horse. Like Tom Faggus's horse the animal was said to be a familiar or even the Devil himself, a reputation not helped by the creature's name of Beelzebub. Kynaston's cave was quite a comfortable residence, Beelzebub had its own stable and Kynaston had a window and an iron door to keep out intruders and law enforcers. When capture threatened Kynaston he could always rely on Beelzebub to outrun their pursuers and return him to the cave.

Legend has it that one day a trap was set for Kynaston, who by this time was earning himself a 'Robin Hood-like' reputation. The local lawmen removed several planks from the Montford Bridge that crossed the river Severn and then lay in wait for the highwayman. When Kynaston arrived he sensed something was wrong and spurred on his horse which made an astounding leap over the missing planks and carried him to safety. On another occasion, Beelzebub is reputed to have jumped from the top of Nesscliffe to Ellesmere, a total distance of nine miles! Furthermore, the horse is said to have jumped a forty-foot-wide section of the Severn at a place still known as Kynaston's Leap. Kynaston eventually received a pardon from Henry VIII and differing accounts tell of how he spent his final years from living in quiet tranquillity, to dying of illness in his cave, or even of moving to Paris. All accounts agree he died in 1534, but legend fails to record what happened to Beelzebub.

THE SPIRIT OF THE HIGHWAYMEN

Many highwaymen came to an early and violent death, either fatally injured during an attempted robbery or hanging at the end of a rope. Perhaps unsurprisingly, their spirits are said to return along with their horses, often it is only because of their steeds that they are known to still roam the area. A ghost story that holds little credence as it involves the fictitious Black Bess, revolves around the murder of two lovers and, of course, Dick Turpin. Legend has it that a house in Bedfordshire called 'Woodfield' was built on the site of a much older property, and that around 200 years ago a father and daughter inhabited the property. The daughter had an illicit affair with a young man; the result being that in a fury the father locked the couple in a cupboard and left them there to die. Some time later, the infamous Dick Turpin broke into the house as part of his usual thieving antics and discovered the remains of the young lovers in the cupboard. Rousing the old man who was still living in the house, he heard the whole sorry tale and blackmailed the man into allowing him to use the house as a hideout.

Dick Turpin, along with the murdered lovers, is still said to haunt the property; a man on horseback is said to have been seen hastily dismounting and rushing into the house through a thick hedge whilst Black Bess is said to be heard galloping down the nearby hill. However, the story's credibility was diminished when, in the last century, the owner of the property attempted to get his rates reduced because of the problem of having a spectral highwayman roaming the grounds.

A more reliable story about a spectral robber and horse involves the famous Lady Catherine Ferrers, one of the few women who took to the road to match their male equivalents at highway robbery. Why Catherine chose this dangerous occupation is not entirely clear, though no doubt like many of her male counterparts it was to bring excitement to an otherwise dull life and to ensure there was always enough money in the household's coffers. Whatever her reason Catherine eventually paid the price for her nightly activities and was shot and mortally wounded during a robbery. She managed to ride home and struggle to the secret room she had created in the house to hide herself, but died at the door. Thus, her secret was finally out, and the room was bricked up. Many witnesses claim to have seen the spirit of Catherine riding her favourite black horse in the grounds, which first appeared at her funeral and was seen 'riding across the treetops'. Sightings have continued to the present day of a mysterious woman in the grounds of her old home.

A GUNLESS WAR OFFICE.

Members of Army Council deliberating. Table littered with papers, in the midst of which reposes a Brodrick cap, which the members have evidently been trying on in turn before a pier-glass in the background, during a discussion as to the responsibility for the introduction of the head-dress in question.

First member (despairingly). No, the thing doesn't suit *any* of us—hardly a fair test perhaps. Wish the thing was in Tibet. Too bad of B. trying to shirk his responsibility for it, after telling me he would approve of anything that wouldn't stop recruiting and be to the taste of the British Nursemaid. Hang the—no, I don't mean that, but it is really most annoying, after all our trouble, that the British Nursemaid should object to the cap. We shall have to get a British Nursemaid on the Council, I suppose.

Second member (impressively, struck by a brilliant idea). There's nothing like testing the matter personally to get at the truth. As a family man you must have a British Nursemaid somewhere on the premises. Now suppose you take the cap home, put it on, have the Nursemaid sent for in a casual, incidental kind of way, and watch the effect.

First member mildly but firmly and decidedly negatives the proposal.

Second member (disappointed). Well, of course if you object, there's no more to be said. By the way, I got an anonymous letter this morning from some fellow who says he knows another fellow who saw an article in an evening paper (an influential evening paper, he says), stating categorically that the guns of the Field Artillery are utterly out of date, and inferior to those of every other European Power—scarce a quick-firer amongst them, except some German guns which we got with great difficulty and in a great hurry when the Boer affair was on; and backs up his statements with the authority of an officer of high rank in the British Army—wonder who that can be? You don't happen to know anything about it? I suppose the public will as usual want to know who is responsible, and how such things are possible after the re-organisation has brought Us into being, and all the rest of it. Why can't these newspaper

follows *and* the public mind their own business! What do they know about our work? Some of 'em would know what work is if they had to design a undress cap! I've got that cap on the brain—rather neat that, eh?—not the cap, but the joke. Well, I dream of that cap all night and think of it all day, and then, on the top of all this, they want to worry us about guns!

First member. Well, I rather fancy, now you speak of it, I *did* hear of something of the kind. They say they've got a splendid gun designed—an 18¼-pounder, a long way the best in the

THE HIGHWAY; OR, THE GHOST'S MISTAKE.

Shade of Turpin. "GADZOOKS! TIMES DON'T SEEM TO HAVE CHANGED MUCH, AFTER ALL!"

market—but they couldn't get the money out of the Treasury, and the manufacturing people actually refuse to make the guns unless they get paid for them —so much for patriotism! But (*with a sudden inspiration*) why not wire down to Woolwich and see if *they* know anything? The KING was down there the other day inspecting the Artillery, and he would have noticed fast enough if there had been anything wrong. Don't believe there is, but perhaps, to satisfy the Public, we might wire, or drop a line to someone down there.

Third Member. Well, we can't possibly see to *everything.* Let's get back to business, or we shall be late for lunch. Now about this cap . . . .

SOME GAS-FREAKS.

A "GREAT GAS EXHIBITION" is to take place shortly at Earl's Court. We understand that among the exhibits and side shows there will be found the following:—

A Set of Fully-Inflated Gas-bags, lent (during the Recess) by the Lower House of Parliament. A large number of these are of Irish manufacture and liable to explode without warning. One of the remainder, a Welsh specimen, is highly-charged and warranted to operate for six hours at a stretch. Another, contributed by a Lancashire firm, is practically inexhaustible. The two latter, with many more of similar construction, will be employed for the illumination of platforms throughout the country pending the approach of the General Election.

Some American "Spell-binders," as used for touring purposes in the West during the recent Presidential campaign. They shed a somewhat garish light, not unmixed with considerable warmth, on impromptu crowds at railway stations, market squares, and other places of public resort.

An Incandescent Mantle, exhibited by the Prophet ELIJAH DOWIE, at white heat by reason of the resistance and non-conductivity of British atmosphere.

A selection of Simple Household Meters (on the Penny-in-the-slot Principle) displayed by the Poet Laureate. They are Made in England, are guaranteed against being "fraud-pilfered," and may be read by a child.

A variety of Safety Burners, otherwise known as "Passive Resisters," very cheap and economical. They are specially designed to lower the rates and at the same time spread the light. Their invention and employment is a liberal education in the art of circumventing the law without burning the fingers. The amount of gas these ingenious little applications give off is simply marvellous.

Manifestos and Orders to the Fleet by Russian admirals, with full directions in the case of Panic at Sea; also a Treatise on "Accidents and How they may be Explained Away."

Manifestos and Orders to the Fleet by British Cabinet Ministers, with complete rules for the diplomatic avoidance of taking offence; also a Text-book on "Pirates at Large, and How their Susceptibilities may be Tenderly Handled."

Dick Turpin and Black Bess are the best-known literary horse and rider, many places even claim to be haunted by the sound of Black Bess' galloping hooves. Unfortunately for them, Black Bess never existed.

In Winchelsea, Sussex, the local spiritual highwaymen are not so keen to reveal themselves. They are believed to be two brothers who lived in the area, George and Joseph Weston, who had adopted assumed names and fooled the local population into believing they were good country gentlemen. Their charade was eventually revealed when they robbed the Bristol Mail and they were apprehended in London, later being hung at Tyburn in the year 1782. Local tradition says they still haunt the roads around their old home. A figure thought to be George (though how anyone can tell because it is claimed he appears headless) is said to be seen waiting beneath a tree for unwary travellers. More disturbing for modern motorists is the sound of a galloping horse approaching their vehicle when there is no animal in sight and then stopping as suddenly as it began.

A highwayman haunting that seems to be only sensed by horses comes from Oxfordshire and involved the father of Sir Julian Paget. His father was returning from a hunt in the years before the First World War and was riding down a sandy lane. His horse stopped sharply and refused to move on though there appeared to be no explanation for its behaviour. He turned the horse around and tried again to move past the spot but every time the horse refused. Puzzlingly, the horse's hoof marks in the sandy ground seemed to form a straight line, going no further than the line of a lone tree in the hedgerow. Finally, not able to make the horse move on, he rode into the field and entered the lane further on and returned to the house he was staying in. He mentioned his strange experience to his host who instantly knew where he meant and remarked that there used to be two trees in the hedgerow opposite each other and that a local highwayman used to string a rope between the two to stop travellers.

Had the horse sensed the spectral presence of the long-departed highwayman? Or, more bafflingly, the ghost of the old rope strung across the roadway? There could be another explanation, it has long been known amongst horsemen that equine's have highly sensitive noses and foul odours will stop a horse in its tracks and cause it to refuse to move. It was an old trick used by horsemen often to cause mischief or to demonstrate their skill over horses. Perhaps there was something on the road that affected the horse's sense of smell? It need not have been deliberately placed; it could have been a natural, but unpleasant smell. A Suffolk ploughman once found that his horses refused to plough across a certain portion of his field no matter how often he tried to get them to move past it, eventually he ploughed the rest of the field and then returned to the spot his horses refused to pass. There he found a dead weasel, the smell of the decaying animal had so struck the horses' sensitive noses that they had been unable to go across that patch of ground.

Whether it was a peculiar odour or a ghost that caused the horse to stop in its tracks, it is a long-standing tradition that horses can sense ghosts, evil and magic. Moreover, while it is most common for horses to appear as an accessory to their riders after death, occasionally ghost horses do return to haunt alone and they are usually unpleasant to meet. One such is a white horse that visited the roads around Epping Forest. The mare would walk out of the trees that lined the road and stand in front of coaches presumably frightening the horses pulling the carriage into halting and only allowing them to move on again once it was given money, which it would carry away into the forest. The horse obtained a semi-mythical reputation, it was said it had a nest in the forest where it stored its treasure and that it gave to the needy. Could there be a logical explanation for the horse? A well-trained animal perhaps that could rob coaches without its owner ever being seen? Certainly it would be a most ingenious robbery scheme. More probably, it was simply a myth or legend that started to circulate, as the creature very rapidly turned into a magical beast and no one appears to have ever been caught for the crimes nor the money ever recovered. Local folklore contends that the horse's treasure is still hidden away in its nest in the woods, but the horse itself appears to have vanished without trace.

HARBINGER HORSES

Like the notorious black hounds that stalk the countryside, frightening lone travellers and bearing ill omen of the future, there are several instances of spectral horses that appear to predict death in a family. The most famous versions of such ill-boding soothsayers are the ghost carriages, drawn by headless horses that are invariably black. Such a device is very commonly used in fiction and is a staple of ghost-lore, but whilst it could be contested that no one has ever truly witnessed such a vision, and that it is purely a figure of folklore and myth, there is no denying that the ghost coach is firmly fixed in the British population's imagination.

The two most famous stories of ghost carriages that are often repeated in great length in ghost books involve the sorrowful figure of Anne Boleyn and the notorious Lady Francis Howard. In the first case, after Anne Boleyn's beheading at Henry VIII's orders, it is said her spirit returns on the anniversary of her death, 19 May, to her birthplace of Blickling Hall (not the current house but an earlier building) riding in a coach pulled by four headless horses and carrying her head in her lap. Like most of these types of tales there are many versions, some say she must cross twenty bridges on Midsummer's Eve at midnight, whilst others contend it is actually her father who must cross the bridges and extend the number to forty.

Similar confusion surrounds the legend of Lady Francis Howard. She was alive in the time of James I and had four husbands, two of which she was reputed to have poisoned. Depending on which version you are familiar with Lady Howard supposedly rides in a carriage made of her dead husbands' bones (or runs alongside it in the shape of a black dog) and approaches Okehampton Castle where she plucks a blade of grass (or in one version a hound plucks it for her) and carries it away. Her nightly visits will only cease when every blade of grass is gone from the grounds of the castle. However, Lady Francis Howard never lived at Okehampton and has no connection to the place, it was a different Lady Howard, Mary, whose family owned the castle and, though she also lived at the time of James I she is not related to the infamous Francis. Due to confusion, the myth has been accidentally relocated to poor Mary and her ancestral home.

It can be seen from these two cases that the headless horses and ghostly coaches are simply local legends told repeatedly until they are confused and distorted. However, why should a spectral coach be a harbinger of death in the first place? This seems unclear though the carriage is always black perhaps suggesting a funeral hearse and often the horses are said to breathe fire, or to having blazing red eyes, or to be headless and invariably black, all signs associated with witchcraft and the Devil. A popular image in the medieval ghost story was a demonic rider hunting down the souls of the wicked on the back of a fiendish black horse, and one of the horsemen of the Apocalypse rides a black horse to bring death and torment to the world. All such imagery no doubt combined to create the phantom coaches we hear of so commonly today, many of the landed gentry used to have a specific coach and four that would come to their home and signal death in the family; some still believe in the tradition today.

However, having just condemned the spectral carriage I should point out that while there can be considered little substance in tales of headless horses, pulling carriages containing headless passengers, particularly those associated with notorious figures and strange punishments in the hereafter, there are examples of actual ghost coaches that are not associated with demonic activities, but simply re-enact an event that took place centuries ago. Joan Forman records such a story in her book *Haunted East Anglia*. The man who observed the ghost was Mr Walker who was driving home shortly after ten at night and was just approaching a stretch of road between Ditchingham and Bungay, where the modern road bypassed an older road, when he saw a carriage pulled by four horses illuminated in his car headlamps. He had time to note the driver on the box of the carriage and the passenger sitting beside him, as well as the two lamps hanging either side of the carriage, before realising he was going to collide with the vehicle. He stopped his car but the carriage came on so he tried to accelerate to get past the coach at which point the horse and carriage veered off onto the old road and, in Mr Walker's words, 'floated away'.

There are many more examples of phantom carriages that exist in the pages of ghost books, some seem to be true hauntings, visions from the past of once-real carriages and their drivers and then there are the bizarre tales of Lady Howard's bone coach and Anne Boleyn's entourage of headless horses. Intriguing though such tales are, horses only play a part in their appearance; they are simply serving the coach driver, pulling the carriage, however, there are some ghost stories where the horse is the sole spectre.

THE SPECTRAL STEED

Ghost horses come in many forms, some are frightening and scare their flesh and blood equivalents, others are simply visitors returning to old pastures and stables and some are even reputed to have saved lives. It seems a common attribute amongst spectral horses that they appear as white, perhaps this is a cultural condition brought on by the belief that white horses could be unlucky, certainly the appearance of these white horses is frightening to those who have encountered them.

A story like this comes from Derbyshire and happened during the first half of the twentieth century. Two women were walking along the Hathersage-Bamford road and had reached a point known as Sicklehome Hollow when one of them saw the terrifying apparition of a white horse appear before her. However, her friend Mrs Hickinson could see nothing, and an argument arose between the women, the one arguing that a horse stood before them, the other equally adamant that there was nothing on the road. In the heat of the argument, the first woman grabbed Mrs Hickinson's arm, whence she immediately was able to see the horse spectre and, argument over, both women hastily left the scene. The explanation for the sudden appearance of the horse is not forthcoming, why it was there and why it appeared before the two women is a mystery.

A bizarre white horse tale that has a hint of mythology about it comes from Pembrokeshire where Oxwick church is supposedly haunted by a phantom white horse that walks about on its hind legs. Local legend gives an explanation to this strange behaviour; several centuries ago it is believed that a form of horse sacrifice was practiced in the area, after the animal was slaughtered its head, neck and forelegs were mounted on a pole and taken down to the coast where they were displayed to scare off invaders. The story is not entirely convincing, such is the nature of most local legends and after all why would a horse wish to come back in the visage it was given after its death? Surely it would rather wander the coast as a normal horse, if wander it does?

An equally peculiar tale is that of Bengie Geare, a former mayor of Okehampton. He must have been considered particularly evil or nasty during his life, for after death it was rumoured he had returned in the shape of a black pony. He haunted Cranmere Pool, in north Dartmoor, a dangerous bog where evil spirits were consigned. It has subsequently been drained and no doubt Bengie Geare's legend along with those of the other evil spirits that occupied the bog were created and circulated to scare people away from such a dangerous place.

Another theoretical evil spirit haunts the glen near Glenarm Castle, Ireland. Supposedly the creature's lair lies beneath rocks near the river and its presence is announced by the noise of galloping horses. Two farm workers who happened to be walking by the river heard the noise and hid behind a bush at the side of the path to see who would appear. Though no one ever came into sight, they heard the galloping hooves approach them, pass them and carry on down the path.

A strange, though not sinister incident happened at a Tudor manor house in Sandford Orcas, Dorset. The property is known to be haunted by a plethora of spirits, but the ghostly horse seems to have only made a singular appearance. The event happened when the property owner's daughter was walking her two bay horses back to the stables, a visitor was in the yard and remarked, 'What a beautiful white horse standing between those two bay ones.' The household did not own a white horse. Simply another puzzling tale without explanation.

Ghosts are supposed to haunt a place because of some tragedy or sudden death that has occurred there. Some consider them to be recordings imprinted into the very fabric of buildings and other locations that are replayed like tape recordings over and over. Such recordings are thought to only occur when there are high levels of emotional energy, such as during a battle, or murder. However, can animals also create such recordings? It is hard to imagine that animals do not have emotions and certainly, they can feel fright, so why should they not too leave behind traces of themselves.

Such an explanation may help us to understand the mysterious spectral pit pony that a Durham miner saw in 1919. Mr T. Gibbon worked in a disused mine, his duty was to descend into the pit at night and relieve the man who worked the electric pumps. Apart from the pumpmen no one ever entered the mine. On New Year's Eve, 1919 Mr Gibbon descended the mine as usual at 9.30 p.m. Following a 500-yard walk along the mine shaft to the pump house he sat down for 'a breather', but was promptly disturbed by a moth that fluttered around his lamp. He chased the moth trying to knock it down with his cloth cap for a distance of about five yards and then had to catch his breath. He found he was at a crossroads and the tunnel directly ahead of him turned to the right and inclined. On his right, a recess was cut into the wall. As he caught his breath in the silent tunnels, he heard the

The white horse features often in ghost stories, possibly because white horses were associated with many superstitions. A spectral white horse appeared to two ladies in Derbyshire and terrified them, though why a white horse should just suddenly appear is unexplained. (Used by permission of the Chapter of Norwich Cathedral)

faint sound of pony hooves and the clatter of the animal's harness and chains. The sound grew closer and then stopped and an arm darted out of the recess on his right and grabbed the bridle of the pony. The pony turned round and retreated back into the mine. Knowing there was no one else in the mine and certainly, no ponies, Mr Gibbon knew he had seen something odd, but it appears not to have worried him, nor prevented him from carrying on with his job.

It was three months later that Mr Gibbon discovered the cause of the ghost. He was talking with the enginewright, wanting to know if any accidents had occurred in that particular mine. The workman told him plainly that a lad was killed down the mine on New Year's Eve, whilst trying to catch a runaway pony. Even later Mr Gibbon had the incident confirmed by another of the miners, who was also a friend; the man not only knew of the death but had also helped carry the boy out of the shaft. It appears Mr Gibbon had witnessed a re-enactment of the runaway pit pony, though whether the arm in the recess belonged to the dead boy or someone else remains unknown.

A story of a gentler nature is told of Nether Lypiatt Manor that was mentioned in chapter eight as being cursed by a blacksmith. The manor is supposed to have several ghosts, as many old houses often do, but the spectral horse 'Wag' is, no doubt, the most interesting. Wag belonged to Judge Coxe who constructed Nether Lypiatt Manor and who also incurred the wrath and subsequent curse of the blacksmith. The horse seems to have been particularly cherished by the volatile judge and an obelisk in the manor's grounds was erected in memory of the animal and a plaque upon it read:

> My name is Wag, that rolled the green,
> The oldest horse that ever was seen,
> My years they numbered forty-two,
> I served my master just and true.

Wag was renowned locally for his good behaviour, tradition states that unattended he would regularly walk down the steep hill into Stroud with panniers on his back. Within these a shopping list was left and Wag would wander to each of the shops and collect the required item before making his way back up the hill. He was also reputed to roll the garden by himself. His spirit is now said to roam the grounds that he knew in life and witnesses have seen a horse charge in through the gates of the manor. Wag clearly remains on the estate in more than just memory.

Finally, mention should be made of a ghost who has hampered jockeys and racehorses on the Newmarket course in Suffolk. The ghost is supposed to be that of Fred Archer, a famous nineteenth-century jockey who won more than 2,000 races in his time. People have witnessed a man resembling Fred on a grey horse riding in the area

This print shows Newmarket racecourses as they would have been in the nineteenth century. Fred Archer, a Victorian jockey, is said to haunt the race track and horses have been known to fall or stop when they come to a point in the course which his ghost is thought to haunt.

of Hamilton Stud Lane. He is also blamed for accidents that occur at a certain point on the Newmarket race course. At this point in the course horses have stumbled, swerved or slowed down for no apparent reason, in 1950 jockey Charlie Smirke was baffled when the horse he was riding, Kermanshah, fell during a race in the same place another horse had fallen only the year before. Both jockeys and spectators have claimed to have seen a strange white shape hovering at this point in the track around the height of a horse's head, and it as widely believed around Newmarket that Fred Archer is still attending the races.

The horse is a many faceted animal; it is a mythological figure, a being capable of seeing things humans cannot, an animal affected by withcraft and magic, yet that can also be magical in itself. The horse has walked alongside man for centuries, no wonder it has become so entwined with our mythology and superstitions. Even today the horse has something majestic about it, something mysterious, perhaps a glint in its eye that suggests intelligence beyond what we already know. They have been loved, used, abused and worshipped, and even today, with cars replacing carriages, tractors replacing hand ploughs, they are still very much part of our world, even if their myth and magic of yesteryear has faded and been forgotten.

BIBLIOGRAPHY

Alexander, Marc *Haunted Castles* (Frederick Muller Ltd 1974)

Ashe, Geoffrey *Mythology of the British Isles* (Methuen 2002)

Askew, Maurice *Hill Figures of England* (The Crowood Press, Wiltshire 2002)

Balchin, Prof. Emeritus W.G.V. (consultant editor) *The Country Life Book of the Living History of Britain* (Country Life Books 1987)

Barber, Richard and Riches, Anne *A Dictionary of Fabulous Beasts* (Macmillan, London Ltd 1971)

Beer, Rudiger Robert *Unicorn: Myth and Reality* (Ash & Grant Ltd 1977)

Blair, John, Keynes, Simon, Lapidge Michael and Scragg, Donald *The Blackwell Encyclopedia of Anglo-Saxon England* (Blackwell Publishing 2003)

Blamires, Steve *The Irish Celtic Magical Tradition – Ancient Wisdom of the Battle of Moytura* (Thorsons 1995)

Borges, Jorge Luis *The Book of Imaginary Beings* (Vintage 2002)

Boria, Sax *The Mythical Zoo* (ABC-CLIO Inc., California 2001)

Briggs, Katherine M. *British Folk Tales and Legends, A Sampler* (Granada Publishing Ltd 1978)

Brown, R. A. *Horse Brasses, Their History and Origin* (Published by Author 1963)

Burke, John *An Illustrated History of England* (Book Club Associates 1974)

Campbell, James *The Anglo Saxons* (Penguin Books 1991)

Cansdale, G.S. *Animals of Bible Lands* (The Paternoster Press 1970)

Carrdus, Kenneth and Miller, Graham *The Search for Britain's Lost Unique Hill Figure* (Published by author 2000/65)

Cavallo, Adolfo Salvatore *The Unicorn Tapestries at the Metropolitan Museum of Art* (The Metropolitan Museum of Art, New York 1998)

Cawthorne, Nigel *The Curious Cures of Old England* (Piatkus Books Ltd 2005)

Cherry, John *Mythical Beasts* (British Museum Press 1995)

Child, Heather and Colles, Dorothy *Christian Symbols: Ancient and Modern* (G. Bell & Sons Ltd 1971)

Clair, Colin *Unnatural History, An Illustrated Bestiary* (Abelard-Schuman 1968)

Cotterell, Arthur *The Encyclopedia of Mythology* (Anness Publishing Ltd 2001)

Curran, Bob *The Creatures of Celtic Myth* (Cassell & Co. 2000)

Daniell, Christopher *Death and Burial in Medieval England 1066-1550* (Routledge 1997)

Daniel, Clarence *Haunted Derbyshire* (The Dalesman Publishing Co. Ltd, North Yorkshire 1975)

Evans, George Ewart *The Horse in the Furrow* (Faber & Faber Ltd 1960)

Evans, George Ewart *Pattern Under the Plough* (Faber & Faber Ltd 1971)

Evans, George Ewart *Horse Power and Magic* (Faber & Faber Ltd 1979)

Ferguson, John and Friar, Stephen *Basic Heraldry* (The Herbert Press 2000)

Frazer, J. G. *The Golden Bough* (Canongate Classics, Edinburgh 2004)

Gallico, Paul *The Steadfast Man: A Life of St Patrick* (Michael Joseph Ltd 1958)

Gotfredsen, Lise *The Unicorn* (The Harvill Press 1999)

Grinsell, Leslie V. *Barrow, Pyramid and Tomb; Ancient Burial Customs in Egypt, the Mediterranean and the British Isles* (Thames & Hudson 1975)

Grinsell, Leslie V. *The Ancient Burial Mounds of England* (Methuen and Co. Ltd 1953)

Hanbury, Zahra and St Aubyn, Astrid *Ghostly Encounters* (Robson Books Ltd 1998)

Hyland, Ann *Equus: The Horse in the Roman World* (B.T. Batsford Ltd 1990)

Hyland, Ann *The Horse in the Middle Ages* (Sutton Publishing Ltd, Gloucestershire 1999)

Joynes, Andrew *Medieval Ghost Stories* (The Boydell Press, Woodbridge 2001)

Lethbridge T. C. *Gogmagog, the Buried Gods* (Routledge & Kegan Paul Ltd 1957)

Mann, Ethel *Old Bungay* (Heath Cranton Ltd 1934)

Marples, Morris *White Horses and other Hill Figures* (Alan Sutton Publishing Ltd, Gloucestershire 1991)

Matthews, Caitlín *The Way of the Celtic Tradition* (Element 2003)

Matthews, John *Tales of the Celtic Otherworld* (Blandford 1998)

Murray, Alexander S. *Manual of Mythology – Greek and Roman Norse and Old German, Hindoo and Egyptian Mythology* (Tudor Publishing Company, New York 1935)

Murray, Gilbert (Translator) *The Hippolytus of Euripides* (George Allen & Unwin Ltd 1922)

Neeson, Eoin *Deidre and Other Great Stories from Celtic Mythology* (Mainstream Publishing Co. Ltd, Edinburgh 1997)

Newman, Paul *Lost Gods of Albion, the Chalk Hill-Figures of Britain* (Alan Sutton Publishing Ltd, Gloucestershire 1997)

Opie, Iona and Tatem, Moira *Oxford Dictionary of Superstitions* (Oxford University Press, 1996)

Orchard, Andy *Cassell's Dictionary of Norse Myth and Legend* (Cassell 1997)

Roud, Steve *The Penguin Guide to the Superstitions of Britain and Ireland* (Penguin Books 2003)

Shepard, Odell *The Lore of the Unicorn* (George Allen & Unwin Ltd 1967)

Slater, Stephen *The Complete Book of Heraldry* (Anness Publishing Ltd 2002)

Taylor, Alison *Burial Practice in Early England* (Tempus Publishing Limited 2001)

Underwood, Peter *The A-Z of British Ghosts* (Chancellor Press 1992)

Underwood, Peter *Ghosts and How to See Them* (Anaya Publishers Ltd 1993)

Water, Colin *A Dictionary of Saints Days, Fasts, Feasts and Festivals* (Countryside Books 2003)

Webber, Ronald *The Village Blacksmith* (David & Charles, Devon 1973)

Wurr, Seelagh *St Aldhelm of Wessex 639 – 709 Bishop of Sherborne 705 – 709* (Bedeguar Books, Warminster, Wiltshire 2004)

Zaczek, Iain *The Book of Irish Legends* (Cico Books 2001)

Bede's Ecclesiastical History of the English Nation (J.M. Dent & Sons Ltd 1930)

Folklore, Myths and Legends of Britain (Reader's Digest Association Ltd 1973)

Encyclopedia of World Mythology (Peerage Books 1975)

Holy Bible, New International Version (Hodder & Stoughton Ltd 1998)

Mystical Rites and Rituals: Initiation and Fertility Rites, Sacrifice and Burial Customs, Incantation and Ritual Magic (Octopus Books Ltd 1975)

Reader's Digest Family Encyclopedia of World History (Reader's Digest Associations Ltd 1996)

Pamphlets and Leaflets

'How to see the White Horses, Uffington and the 8 in Wiltshire' (Compiled and Published by J. & M. Young, Wiltshire)

'Welcome to Wandlebury Country Park and Nature Reserve' (Cambridge Preservation Society)

Buchanan, Ronald H. (Ulster Folklife, Volume 2 1956 'A Buried Horse Skull')

Harris, K.M. (Ulster Folklife, Volume 3 1957 'Buried Horse Skulls: A Further Note')

Harris, K.M. (Ulster Folklife, Volume 4 1958 'More Buried Horse Skulls')